Born to Fly

Also by Sara Evans

Love Lifted Me

Softly & Tenderly

The Sweet By & By

Born to Fly

A MEMOIR

SARA EVANS

HOWARD BOOKS

ATRIA

New York   London   Toronto   Sydney   New Delhi

HOWARD BOOKS

ATRIA

An Imprint of Simon & Schuster, Inc.
1230 Avenue of the Americas
New York, NY 10020

First Howard Books hardcover edition September 2020

HOWARD BOOKS/**ATRIA** B O O K S and colophon
are trademarks of Simon & Schuster, Inc.

For information about special discounts for bulk purchases, please contact Simon & Schuster Special Sales at 1-866-506-1949 or business@simonandschuster.com.

The Simon & Schuster Speakers Bureau can bring authors to your live event. For more information or to book an event, contact the Simon & Schuster Speakers Bureau at 1-866-248-3049 or visit our website at www.simonspeakers.com.

Interior design by Kyoko Watanabe

Manufactured in the United States of America

1 3 5 7 9 10 8 6 4 2

Library of Congress Cataloging-in-Publication Data

Names: Evans, Sara, 1971- author.
Title: Born to fly : a memoir / Sara Evans.
Identifiers: LCCN 2020012711 (print) | LCCN 2020012712 (ebook) |
ISBN 9781501162589 (hardcover) | ISBN 9781501162640 (ebook)
Subjects: LCSH: Evans, Sara, 1971- | Singers—United States—Biography. |
Country musicians—United States—Biography. | LCGFT: Autobiographies.
Classification: LCC ML420.E957 A3 2020 (print) | LCC ML420.E957 (ebook) |
DDC 782.421642092 [B]--dc23
LC record available at https://lccn.loc.gov/2020012711
LC ebook record available at https://lccn.loc.gov/2020012712

ISBN 978-1-5011-6258-9
ISBN 978-1-5011-6264-0 (ebook)

I dedicate this book to my family. My whole family. Parents, siblings, children, and my husband. I also dedicate it to my closest friends. You know who you are.

This book is just a snippet of my entire story, but it felt like the right time to tell some of it.

Contents

PART ONE

Then

CONTENTS

PART TWO

Now

PART ONE

Then

Chapter 1

BIG FARMHOUSE ON THE PRAIRIE

Drama has been a part of my life since my birth. I was not just a breech baby, I was trying to come out butt first! I mean, it's just so typical that I would do that! What an ass!

My mom says that she had to walk the hallways of the hospital for hours to get me to turn the right way so I could enter this world. It's true, I've always wanted to be the center of attention. That is a great picture of how I have been my whole life and still am to this day. I *love* being the center of attention. It's how I am wired. But it's not like I'm a narcissist or anything. I just love to entertain people. I love to tell a good story and make people happy. It makes total sense that my mother put me on stage when I was four years old. I've been entertaining people ever since.

I'm a Midwestern girl. I grew up in New Franklin, Missouri—a Middle American town with mostly conservative family values. It's one of those places where people work hard their entire lives, often with very little to show for it. My hometown sits in the center of the state and is a farming community of about a thousand people. That population has hardly changed in a hundred years, and that's no exaggeration. The land is rolling countryside and wooded hills covered in oaks, elms, and dogwood trees. Rivers and streams are everywhere, and then, of course, we have the great Missouri, North America's longest river, making its vast journey along seven states until finding its end at the Mississippi River near St. Louis. Simply put, New Franklin is in a gorgeous part of America.

Even today, it's a town where everybody knows everybody. There were just thirty-five kids in my graduating class. I would say I was popular in high school for sure, but I was just a simple farm girl and I didn't come into my own until after high school. I had no style. Everyone was basically the same. No one really had a lot of money, and we all wore boots and Levi's and t-shirts to school. I did the best I could to be cute, but I didn't think I was beautiful really until I reached my early twenties. And that meant learning what real beauty was. More on that later . . .

My childhood was spent riding horses, riding motorcycles, playing pretend, and just being a happy little girl. I loved growing up on a farm. And I always had a strong love of hard physical labor. I've never been afraid to work hard. I'm so much like my mom in that way.

When I was four years old, my parents, my two older brothers, and I moved to my mom's dream home—a huge old yellow house built in the 1800s, on a four-hundred-acre farm. The house had not been lived in for years when we moved in, and it needed a ton of work. My mother works harder than anyone I've ever known, and even though she was pregnant with my sister Lesley and already had three young children, she dove into remodeling the place, at the same time trying to get the whole farm in working order and fighting an infestation of black snakes. This is a type of snake that is not poisonous but can grow to be eight to ten feet long. And they WILL BITE YOU!!!!! Every day that first summer, we killed at least five snakes with a garden hoe. We have so many snake stories from that house. First of all, when we moved in and started exploring the huge yards, we noticed that they were literally hanging from the trees! So we started shooting at them with BB guns. I actually got so good that I could shoot a hanging snake from a good ten feet away. One time my mom was sitting on the toilet and she looked up and a black snake was climbing down the wall right in front of her. She just calmly got up and got a broom and swept the snake outside.

Unlike most people, who scream and run when they see a snake, my mother is not afraid of them—or of anything, for that matter! The rest of us were terrified, like normal people, and I still am terrified of snakes today. But mom's fearlessness, combined with her sense of humor, made life interesting. Mom once killed a black snake, wound it in a circle, wrapped it up, and hid it in the helmet my dad kept on the seat of his beloved motorcycle. So when he lifted the helmet up to put it on, a huge dead snake uncoiled and fell out onto the ground. We were all watching from inside the house through the big window in the front room. It scared the crap out of him and probably infuriated him. It would have made me so mad. But he was a pretty good sport about it. He knew that was just my mom's sense of humor, and he eventually laughed about it too. Mom would do things like chase us around the living room with a dead spider that she had just killed, laid out on a paper towel. We would be screaming bloody murder and she would be dying laughing. I think it was her way of trying to toughen us up. I know this sounds so mean, but it really wasn't. My mother is just like that. She is literally the smartest and funniest person I've ever known.

I was definitely a daddy's girl. He and I bonded over a shared love of singing, and until I was four years old, I was the only girl and the youngest child. So naturally I received a lot of attention. And just because I was so stinking adorable! I was also the first granddaughter on my mom's side, so Granny and Papa (pronounced "Pawpaw") favored me too. I'm sure of it.

When I'd hear the sound of Dad's motorcycle coming up the gravel driveway, I'd tear into the living room as the front door swung open. Dad would see me and start singing, "Weeeelllllll, heeeelllllllll-O, Dolly! Well, hello, Dolly, it's so nice to be back home where I belong."

He'd pick me up and swing me around as he continued the dramatic theme song to the Broadway show *Hello, Dolly!* For some reason, "Dolly" was one of my nicknames. And then it turned into Dobbish. We are strange.

Other times when our family was loading up to visit Grandpa and Grandma Evans's farm down in the Missouri River bottom, Dad would call from across the yard.

"Hey, Sara, wanna ride with me?"

The truth is, I really wanted to ride with him, but I was also a bit terrified of riding with him, because he went really, really fast, and we lived on a winding, dangerous country highway with a lot of sharp turns. He would take those turns like a man on a motorcycle is supposed to—going all the way down to the right knee for a right turn and all the way to the left knee for a left turn. And you know how it is when you are NOT the one in control of the vehicle. It's terrifying. So my instinct was to lean the opposite way from the way he was leaning. I knew those roads like the back of my hand, so I would prepare myself for the next sharp curve. It made him very angry, and one time he pulled the bike over and said, "What are you doing? Stop doing that! You're going to cause us to wreck! Just sit still!" I don't think he meant to be quite that harsh with me, but it hurt my feelings so badly because he'd never been that way with me before. I cried the rest of the way there, with my arms wrapped around his waist and my face cradled into his black leather jacket. But when we got to Grandma and Grandpa's house, I pretended nothing was wrong.

I have always said that if I could trade places with anyone in the world, I would choose each of my children for a few days so that I could know what they think of me, of their lives, of themselves, and if they are truly happy. There were several things like the motorcycle story that happened when I was little that really hurt my feelings and have sort of stayed with me my whole life. And I had very loving parents. I just think that we need to be so careful that we don't hurt our children's feelings, and if we do, we need to apologize to them. Because let's be honest, we all know when we've said or done something to hurt someone's feelings, and we all can be prideful about it and not want to apologize. But when it's your own child, you have to say you're sorry.

One time on a hot and muggy Missouri summer day, I was outside playing in a little plastic pool that we got at Walmart, and I had been making up this song to surprise my mom when she came out. When I saw her and my brother in their rubber boots headed to the hog barn to feed, I said, "Mommy, come here, I want to show you something!" They walked over to me and I sang this little song for them, and at the very end I splashed them with the pool water. My mom got so annoyed that she took it out on me. I'm sure there were probably other things going on that were stressing her out that I didn't have a clue about. I'm not sure why that has stuck with me all these years. I think it's because my intention was to make her happy with my little song, and I wasn't trying to be irritating. So when she walked away, I was left stunned and incredibly hurt. I don't tell this story to try to make my parents sound mean. They weren't. They were very loving and fun, and we were happy up until a certain point. No, I tell that story to remind you parents and myself that you have to be so careful with your kids' hearts. And if you feel you've been too harsh, or hurt them because of something else that's going on, make sure you tell them you're sorry and that it's not them, it's you.

I've always been accident-prone. After moving to the farm, right off the bat I disobeyed my parents and did something really, really stupid, which earned me the nickname Crisco (another one of many). A lot of people today won't understand that joke, but Crisco shortening is the essential ingredient in flaky biscuits and piecrusts.

A Missouri farm kid

In other words, I was a total flake. I was FLAKY—that's why they called me Crisco. Get it? Now I know that I was just creative and always daydreaming.

There was a large open hole in the front yard that needed to be filled and covered. It looked like a deep well, but it was actually a septic tank. I was riding around the yard on my tricycle while my parents were cutting branches down from the trees with a chain saw. Mom told me at least five hundred times to stay far away from that hole. So what did I do? I decided to ride backward on my tricycle around the yard because, well, just because. Why does any four-year-old do anything? And who lets their four-year-old ride a tricycle unattended near a deep and deadly open septic tank while running a chain saw! So of course, I backed right into the hole! I remember going under and trying to pull myself out by grabbing blades of grass while screaming at the top of my lungs for help. My parents couldn't hear me because, like I said, they were running the chain saw!!!!!!!

Mercifully, they stopped cutting and heard my screams, ran to the hole, and pulled me out. I can only imagine how it must have felt for my mom and dad to race to their only daughter down a hole full of poop. I literally smelled like a Porta Potty for days, even after hours and hours of bathing!

∞

It wasn't long after we'd moved to the farm that my first sister, Lesley, was born. I was so excited to be a big sister! I loved helping Mom take care of her, spooning in her first bites of food, cheering as she rolled over, and crawling beside her once she could get around the room. Having younger siblings, especially having much younger siblings, no doubt helped me be a better mom once I started my own family. My two half sisters are fourteen and eighteen years younger than I am, so I felt like I had already raised two kids when my first child, Avery, was born. (That didn't make it any less terrifying when I brought him home from the hospital, though.)

Farming is a family affair. On those four hundred acres, we raised cattle and hogs and grew a variety of crops. Our family grew as well. My younger sisters, Lesley and Ashley, born four and six years after me, made us a family of seven. We all learned to work hard from an early age. We never considered that we had a choice whether to work or not, because we didn't. The boys were usually working outside with Mom and any hired help we could afford, while my sisters and I did both house and farm work.

Spring was planting time, and summers were spent in the fields tending the crops and caring for the animals. Sometimes the cows would break through a fence or one might wander off and I'd have to saddle my horse and help find it and get it safely back to the barn. Autumn was the harvest, and the boys and I helped as soon as we were home from school.

Even with the entire family participating, farming didn't bring in enough to pay the bills. My dad started working the late shift at the *Columbia Daily Tribune* as a pressman in Columbia, Missouri, and Mom drove the school bus mornings and afternoons—a job she held for a little over forty years until retiring just recently.

My mother cared for all the practical details of our lives, making three home-cooked meals a day, taking on side jobs whenever she could, and generally making our home a comfortable haven. Because of my mother, I have strong family values, and I believe in the importance of cooking for your family, not eating out every night. I love to cook for my family, and I repeat many of those recipes passed down from Granny and my mom.

Even if it was brutally exhausting, and overwhelming at times,

Mom's dream came true when we moved to the farm. The earth called to something deep inside of her. It's something I fully understand. If I hadn't become a musician, I'd surely be living on and working my own farm today.

As it happens, though, I was born with a God-given gift for music. This became apparent when my two older brothers started taking guitar lessons. As they were learning, I would come in and start singing. And I was good. I was really good. I could literally sing anything, and I was only four years old. Funny that I couldn't obey a simple order not to ride my tricycle near a dangerous and deadly open septic tank, but I could sing beautifully, and learn lyrics and harmonies, and I could understand music theory on a higher level than a four-year-old should be able to.

My mom's strong entrepreneurial spirit gave her the idea to put a band together.

We started learning songs by people like Loretta Lynn, Crystal Gayle, Patsy Cline, Reba McEntire, Patty Loveless, the Eagles, Barbara Mandrell, Ronnie Milsap, and many more. I started playing the mandolin as well.

Both of my parents were musical themselves, but performing didn't appeal to them. They were happy to listen to us perform instead. My mother even turned the formal living room into the "music room." It was soon filled with guitars, microphones, amps, cords, and stereo equipment. And that's where we became musicians. We didn't always love it, because there were many times that we wanted to lie around and watch TV, but my mom would make us practice whenever we had free time on the farm. And thank God she did.

One of my best memories is of singing with my dad. We'd sing together on the faded couch in the living room, songs like "Heaven's Just a Sin Away" from the Kendalls—a father-and-daughter duo. I would belt out the lead parts and my dad would sing harmony with me. I cry just thinking about those days. Everyone started to believe that I might be a prodigy, and that my brothers might be, too. My sisters would eventually show the same exact talent.

Before long, we were traveling all over Missouri playing at fairs, festivals, rodeos, wedding dances, senior citizen homes, Eagles Lodge dances, and eventually bars and dance halls (pretty much exactly what I do today, but strike senior citizen homes and add casinos and arenas).

I remember loving the reaction on people's faces when they heard me sing. In the movie *Sweet Dreams,* Patsy Cline says something like, "When I'm on stage and I look in people's faces, I can tell that I've reached right down into their souls with my voice." That is exactly how I feel every time I'm on stage. It's an indescribable feeling, and a high that lasts for hours after every concert.

Before long, my brothers and I were local celebrities. People would say, "Have you heard the Evans kids? They're really good, and that little Sara can sing anything." So at the age of five, my professional music career had begun. By age six, I was fronting the Evans Family Band. My brother Jay played guitar, my brother Matt played bass, and I sang lead and played the mandolin. I suppose the acclaim could've gone to our heads, but it just didn't. Being poor and working hard on the farm kept us humble. Our music brought us attention, and that was great, but our band helped support the family as well.

Then when I was eight years old, something happened that would put everything on hold.

Chapter 2

THE ACCIDENT

June 29, 1979, is a day that will be etched in our memories until we die. Around 5:30 p.m. my mom, my brother Jay, and a hired guy were working on a tractor that had broken down out by the barn. My little sisters were in the house playing, and my brother Matt was watching TV. Dad was in the shower getting ready to go to work at the *Tribune*. It seemed like just another lazy summer afternoon.

All day I had been playing pretend with my dolls on the wraparound porch that I'd turned into my playhouse. This part of the porch was off the side of my parents' bedroom, and I spent hours alone there, playing house with my dolls all lined up or tucked into little beds. I played wife and mom doing wife-and-mom duties like instructing my babies in how to behave, cooking Sunday dinner, or hanging their little dresses on a makeshift clothesline. I often sang along to an Emmylou Harris record and would race inside to the record player when the album ended. I'd climb up a stool and move the needle back to start the record over again. I'd watch the slight roll of the vinyl as it turned, listen to the scratchy sound of the needle as it began its journey back to the center. Then I'd race back to my babies as Emmylou's voice filled the house again.

Just a few days earlier, I had decided that part of my pretend mommy duties included getting the mail. Our mailbox was at the end of our long gravel driveway and on the other side of the country highway. I knew I'd get in trouble for going down there alone if I got caught, but once I got something in my mind there was no stopping me.

I was just as much a tomboy as I was a girlie girl, being that I was the first daughter, with two older brothers. I played sports, and I also took ballet lessons. I played with Barbie dolls, and I rode a motorcycle. I rode horses, and I had slumber parties with my girlfriends. That's the kind of girl I was, but one thing I loved most was my motorcycle. It wasn't a small bike—it took all of my eight-year-old strength to roll it out to the driveway and kick-start it. Then I'd hop on and rev up the engine. We all had motorcycles—well, at least my brothers, my dad, and I all did. Jay and Matt both had Hodaka bikes. Jay had a Dirt Squirt and Matt had a Road Toad, and Dad had a Yamaha Virago. Mine was a Yamaha 80 that I was so proud of and loved to my core, because what eight-year-old girl has her own motorcycle to ride?

My mom said if I wasn't with my brothers, the farthest I could go was up and down the driveway near the house and down to the pond. I wasn't supposed to cross the highway or even get near it, not ever. I figured I could do it without anyone seeing me.

My first trip to the mailbox was uneventful, and no one saw me do it. I remember the wind in my face and feeling invincible while heading down the driveway to get the mail. I felt grown-up and proud of myself, and I didn't tell anyone—especially not my brothers, who would've told on me.

On this day, I remember putting together an outfit of my own design. When you're poor and don't have a lot of clothes, you have to be creative. For Easter, Granny had given me a cute little pink-and-white shorts outfit. I decided the top would be even cuter with some cutoff denim shorts that my mom had made for me. And then I put on my new white Nike tennis shoes that I had also gotten for Easter. These were all such valuable items, as I knew it would be months before I got something else new. Much later, that outfit would come home from the hospital in a bag, covered in blood.

Once I reached the end of the driveway, I got off my motorcycle, stood by the highway, and waited. I looked to the left, looked to the right, and saw no cars. I did hear a car in the distance, but I thought I could make it across the road before it got to me. The last thing I remember was seeing a flash of blue to my left.

I woke up in a cold sterile room and then came the pain, just pain.

I was terrified and had no idea where I was or what had happened to me. Both of my legs were in casts, and my arms were bound. Outside the window, it was dark. I immediately started screaming and crying.

A nurse ran in to try to comfort me and calm me down. She asked, "Sara, do you remember what happened to you?"

"No," I said.

"You were hit by a car."

It didn't make sense, and I just kept asking for my mommy. "Where's my mom, I want my mommy!!!"

The nurse told me that my mom had just left to go shower and get some rest at Granny's house. I never wanted anything so much in all my life as I wanted my mother at that moment. The most shocking part of this story is that they wouldn't call her. I suppose the nurse thought I'd fall back to sleep or that my mother needed some rest, but that was a horrible decision on her part. For the next several hours, I stared out the window in agony, waiting for the sun to come up, because that's when they said she'd come back. My mom's younger brother, Uncle Dale, was in the cafeteria when I woke up. They called him in, so at least I had someone I knew, but all I wanted was my mom.

The next time I woke up, my mom was there. She looked like she'd been through hell and back. She began to tell me what had happened.

∞

Highway 89 is the road that runs in front of our farm. It's hilly and treacherous. There have been many accidents on that highway, some fatal. Years later, at almost the same spot where I got hit, we witnessed a horrible wreck and the death of someone we knew well. Our driveway was at the bottom of two big hills. The woman who hit me was going seventy-five miles an hour. When she came over the hill, I was standing in the road and she couldn't stop. The only thing I can guess is that once I reached the middle of the highway and saw the car, I froze in panic and it was too late for her to do anything other than hit me.

When the car struck me, I was thrown onto the hood. There was a huge dent where my head hit the hood of her car. When she slammed on her brakes, I was thrown off the car and into the air before I landed eighty feet off the road in a ditch with tall grass.

The woman lived in the area, and her son who was in the car was in the same grade as my brother. They immediately turned around and drove back to our driveway. The son got out and ran beside the car yelling, "We hit Sara! We hit Sara!"

When my mom heard them shouting, she kicked off her flip-flops and ran barefoot down our gravel driveway to get to me. Have you ever run barefoot on gravel? It hurts like hell. I didn't get that part fully until I became a mother, and now it's one of my favorite parts of the story. Like her, I would run barefoot across broken glass if my child needed me.

At first, no one could find me. The grass was high along the roadside, and no one expected that I'd be eighty feet off the road. When they found me, I was curled up in a ball with my left leg mangled and twisted and almost severed in two. They all thought I was dead.

Mom sent the hired hand back to the house to tell my dad. He called the ambulance, then he and Matt ran down to the road. Then Mom sent Jay and Matt to the neighbors' house for help. Out in the country, a "neighbor" is up the road on a huge farm of their own. They aren't right next door. If you turned right out of our driveway, our neighbors were up a long hill, and their house was also at the end of a long driveway. The boys ran as fast as they could to the neighbors' front door and collapsed to the floor, shouting, "Sara's been hit by a car!" I cannot even imagine how scared my brothers were while running all that way to get help and thinking their little sister was most likely dead. As soon as our neighbors, who were also close family friends, understood what the boys were saying, they started rallying everyone they could think of to call. Word traveled quickly, and before long there were cars and farm trucks lined up for miles down the road. People came to help.

Forty-five minutes later, the ambulance came screeching up the road, weaving around cars till it came to a stop. I was still unconscious, but at least by then, they knew I was alive.

The EMTs put rubber casts around my legs and took me to the hospital in Boonville. My injuries were too severe for them to handle, so they sent me to the hospital at the University of Missouri in Columbia, about thirty miles away.

I had a severe concussion and had been unconscious for almost two days before I finally woke up in pain. Mom finished telling me what had happened, but I couldn't quite take it all in. It was about to get even worse.

A young, handsome man named Dr. Breedlove, probably just out of medical school, came in and told my mom that my left leg needed pins put in immediately. The problem was that since my concussion was so serious, they were afraid to put me under anesthesia. The room went silent as the reality of what he was saying set in.

He went on to explain that the procedure would go like this: They'd give me local anesthesia to try numbing my leg as much as possible, and then he would use a hand drill to get the pin into my left knee. It was a difficult decision, because he felt sure that if we didn't put the pin in, I would have a deformed leg for the rest of my life. And I don't know if you've ever seen my legs, but repairing them was the right decision! I have great gams!

My dad was at work, so my mom's father, Papa Floyd, said he would stay in the surgery room with my mom. I remember the nurses on either side of me, holding me down as Dr. Breedlove picked up the drill. Every time he brought the drill close to my leg, I cried out, saying, "Wait, wait, wait!" I just couldn't let him do it. I was absolutely terrified. I mean, imagine someone wanting to drill a pin in your leg while you're lying there wide awake. But after my several attempts to stop the inevitable, Dr. Breedlove finally just told the nurses to hold me down so he could get it over with.

∞

As soon as the drill hit my leg, the pain sent me into shock, and I mercifully passed out. I didn't wake up for ten hours. My mom told me later that Dr. Breedlove was so upset and probably traumatized that he said, "I will never, ever do that again."

When I woke this time, my mom was there. I looked down, and my body looked like Wile E. Coyote's after a run-in with the Road Runner, but no one was laughing. My left leg was in traction, with pulleys, weights, and cables hanging at my feet. The cables had to be adjusted several times a day, and pain would shoot through my ankle all the way to my head. My right side was in a full cast from my hip to my toes. Both of my arms were sprained and bound.

For six agonizing weeks, I remained in that hospital bed.

As an eight-year-old who loved to run free and wild, it was pure torture being strapped down, hardly able to move, and in pain nearly all of the time. Also knowing that my whole summer was passing me by . . . I couldn't swim or do anything fun—well, talk about feeling sorry for myself. I got through each day with the help of the sweet nurses and staff at the hospital and all the amazing people in my life. As soon as the news of the accident spread, and it was covered in all our local media, I was inundated with gifts, money, and stuffed animals from family, friends, and people in the community.

My family and friends also coordinated shifts to spend time with me. With my dad working most nights, and a farm to run, my mom couldn't always be with me. My mother was only thirty-two years old at this time, and she had five kids. I just can't imagine the stress that she was under. Every evening, Granny and Papa Floyd came to visit me, and Granny brought me fried chicken. Granny's love language was acts of service, with a strong emphasis on cooking, and I loved fried chicken with mashed potatoes and gravy. I'd ask for it all the time, and I was so spoiled and clearly her favorite (my siblings may disagree) that Granny brought it every single night.

"Brought your favorite!" she'd say as she walked into my hospital room with a smile. Granny and Papa Floyd would stay with me during that cozy evening time until visiting hours were over. To me, from around 5:00 p.m. till bedtime is the BEST time of any day. It could very well be because that's when Granny and Papa would come to the hospital and I would eat dinner and they would sit with me and watch TV or just talk to me. It made me feel so safe and loved.

But being in the hospital really was unbelievably boring. And there were like two channels on the crappy TV they had. I remember it seemed like *M*A*S*H* was the ONLY thing on at all times. Every time the theme song would come on I would get so sad. I've always been very affected by music. Later I learned that the name of the song is "Suicide Is Painless," and I'm like, "Well, of course it depressed the crap out of me!" I didn't particularly like the show anyway. I was too young to understand it and I didn't get why people seemed happy to be in Korea.

My brother Jay seemed particularly traumatized by my accident. It truly was a horrific accident, and we were all aware of the miracle it was that I survived. And I was his little sister and he adored me, so he volunteered to stay many of the nights at the hospital, sleeping on a little couch bed on the side of the room. In the night when I needed help with something, I'd call out for him, but he was a very sound sleeper.

"Jay! Wake up, Jay!" The end of my bed was absolutely covered with the stuffed animals that people had brought, and I would throw them one at a time at him until he woke up and helped me. He and I spent hours doing crossword puzzles, reading, and watching *M*A*S*H*. I was so touched and moved by his concern for me that I didn't want to say anything about it for fear of embarrassing him. So I just tried to play it cool. But I will never forget how upset he was over the whole thing.

A few times over those six weeks, I'd have a sudden, overwhelming feeling of pain and panic consuming me. "I want out of this!" I'd

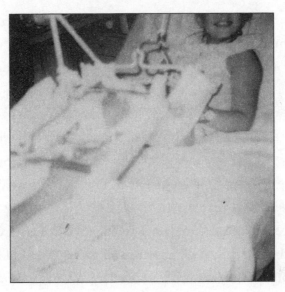

Smiling through the pain

scream, thrashing around till someone held me down and calmed me. I felt like I was being buried alive and couldn't move to get out. It made me so claustrophobic, and I still am very much so today. I can't stand to feel trapped or confined. I'm terrified of elevators—not elevators themselves but being trapped in one. Honestly, if I were to ever get trapped in an elevator, I don't know how I would cope. Or if I would cope. Just talking about the idea of being trapped inside that confined space makes me start sweating and makes my heart race. If someone even pretends to hold me down and not let me move, I will scream bloody murder. I'm no psychologist, but I would guess that being in traction in a hospital bed for six weeks without getting up one time, and then being in two full casts on both legs for another year, would make anyone claustrophobic. And contribute to several other issues in the anxiety category.

My parents promised me little surprises and special things to help me look forward to getting released. "We'll go get pizza. You can spend the night with Granny and Papa when you get out, we'll have a big fish fry and all the relatives will come over, you can have a slumber party . . ."—things like that. My mom also promised that I'd get a cute new outfit to wear home. This sparked a search back through the JCPenney catalog. I finally settled on this green-and-white striped velour shorts outfit that looked like something Chrissy Snow would wear on the TV show *Three's Company*. I loved it! I would be styling in that wheelchair with casts on my legs!

Granny and Papa also told me I could pick out a gift from the catalog, so I chose a baby doll. It arrived about two weeks into my stay in the hospital. She was so cute. I kept her beside me in my bed at all times. When it came time for my last surgery to get the pins out of my left leg before sending me home—my right leg was still in a full cast—the doctor put casts on my baby's legs, too. I woke from the surgery to see her beside me, and I was so excited. My doll and I both went home with casts on our legs. Such a sweet thing for that doctor to do.

Pain changes people. It can shape a life for the good, or twist and turn it in a bad way. For me, pain came with the side effect of awakening. Somewhere in the pain, the glaring boredom of an active child confined not just to a room but her own body, and the culmination of trauma of those weeks in that hospital—this awakening developed my eight-year-old mind.

My parents had always taken us to church and Sunday school. I knew the Bible stories and believed that God was real. But I didn't think about God outside of church. We were a good, honest, hardworking family who went to church on Sundays, but that was about it when it came to God. Yet nearly every day I had visitors at the hospital, and someone invariably brought Him up. Family, friends, and church members would come in to visit me, and their words touched that *something* growing inside my heart.

"The Lord was really looking after you, Sara."

"Oh, honey, you are so lucky to be alive. God must have a very important purpose for you."

"God did a miracle in you. Don't you forget that, not ever."

And suddenly, I believed it.

I developed an understanding that God did have a purpose for me. It settled in as something I just knew to be true. I had this sense that I'd never be down for long or alone, no matter what I faced, because God was with me. He saved my life for a reason.

This felt like a special light in my heart or a fire for the Lord and for other people. I had a purpose in life, and I knew that God allowed me to survive that horrible accident, and I wanted to make him proud of me. So I needed to find out what that purpose was and never take it for granted.

My body healed slowly, but my spirit was soaring.

Since then, I've had a compelling desire to be a good person, to be the best I can be for everyone I encounter, to improve my situation, to improve the lives of others with kindness and generosity, and to be the living example of Christ so that others will want to seek a relationship with Him.

When I was released from the hospital after six weeks, in some ways, the work was just beginning. I spent the next two years in casts, having surgeries, going to doctor's appointments, having physical therapy. I started third grade in a wheelchair. I can't imagine the strain that put on my family, especially with my two sisters being just two and four years old.

I struggled a ton with anxiety from PTSD (post-traumatic stress disorder). I developed unreasonable fears about dying in my sleep. I was afraid I would go blind. I was in physical pain most of the time. And I wasn't the only one in pain. My parents were struggling, too. They were extremely worried about me and trying to balance hospital visits, work, the farm, and my older and younger siblings. Then the hospital bills started coming in the mail. It was almost too much to ask of anybody. I think that's when my parents started to grow apart from stress.

But even with the pain and fears and struggles, I knew without a doubt that God was real and He'd never leave me. For you reading this, I hope you'll experience something like this as well. Not a near life-ending accident, of course, but a complete understanding of the fact that God wants to be in your life and that He has a calling for you. He's always providing and protecting. And HE LOVES US.

As my body began to heal, my heart and soul were calling me back to music. Before long, we put the band back together and started doing shows. I even performed in a wheelchair, and believe me, that tip jar was full at the end of the night.

And at the age of eight years old, I knew that music was my calling. The accident taught me so much about patience and perseverance. When you endure hard things, you get stronger. There were many more challenges ahead, but my purpose on this earth has been clear ever since. I knew that I had a purpose, and that I would not ever let anything stop me from fulfilling it.

Chapter 3

THE BEST MEDICINE

I grew up in a home that was full of laughter. As hard as we worked, we laughed even harder. My siblings and I have family stories that we tell and retell whenever we get together, and we laugh no matter how many times we tell them.

One of many stories is how on some Friday nights after Dad came home from work, Mom or Dad would call out to us five kids, saying, "We're going to Dairy Queen, let's go!"

We'd cheer and run around grabbing shoes and brushing our hair real fast, then we'd climb into the back of our big silver van and head to town. Boonville, Missouri, to be specific. The silver van . . . it was awesome. On long trips we even pulled out the seats so we could make a pallet and sleep. We had all these cassettes and eight-track tapes to pick from. We'd recline against a few pillows and listen to music when we drove anywhere. One of my favorites was Ronnie

Milsap's *Greatest Hits*. I'd pass it up for Mom to put into the tape deck, and then we'd sing together, songs like "Let's Take the Long Way Around the World" and "Smoky Mountain Rain."

A trip to Dairy Queen was special. And for me, it had become more special because I had discovered the very best malt known to man, but it wasn't "technically" on the menu. It was a peanut butter malt. Perhaps you've heard of it. It's a regular chocolate malt with the perfect amount of peanut butter. I think I heard about it from a friend who said she had gotten one recently and it was to die for. Jay was the oldest in our big family. He got a lot of special treatment, but he also had more responsibilities sometimes, like being the one who had to go into DQ and order for everyone. So after our arrival, Jay would get out of the van and stand at the open door waiting for our orders. And in typical teenager fashion, he was slightly grumpy at all times. Hormones.

One night, I asked for a peanut butter malt, and when he went in to order it, the cute teenage girl working there looked at him and probably in her best Valley Girl voice said, "Excuse me? Um, like, we don't like have, like, peanut butter malts. I'll, like, have to, like, ask my manager . . ." I'm picturing her pulling her gum out in a long strand and curling it around her forefinger. Well, that humiliated Jay, and he vowed that he would NEVER order me a peanut butter malt ever again.

But the next time we went to DQ, I was still dreaming of the PB malt. I couldn't stop thinking about it! And you can imagine Jay was thinking about that cute girl behind the counter. As usual, Jay was commissioned to go in and get everything. Everyone went around telling their orders, but he wouldn't look at me until the very end, when I said, as fast as I could, "Peanutbuttermalt." All one word. I was so scared, but not scared enough not to try. He threw his head back and said, "Mom! Why do I have to get that for her? It's not even on the freaking regular menu!" But we all knew why it really made him mad, so my mom joined the fun. "Jay, just order it, it's not a big deal," she said, trying to hide her grin.

That's how we were raised. To be funny and tease one another and laugh at ourselves. I don't think anyone should take themselves too seriously or be too defensive. It's quite annoying and shows insecurity. My mom taught us to laugh at ourselves and allow loved ones to show us when we are being asses, and it was very effective. We would be having a big Sunday dinner with extended family over and my mom would say, right in front of me, "Oh, guess what happened with Sara this weekend . . ." And the whole family would know whatever stupid thing I had done to get myself in trouble, and they would weigh in and it would become a family talk. But often it was very helpful, and it definitely made our family closer. I'm all about being open and transparent. I know families who try to hide all of their faults and keep secrets from each other, and it's very toxic. Families should be there for each other and should know what's going on with everyone so that they can help each other.

We love laughing at ourselves but sometimes things are the opposite of funny, here's a story that will go down in infamy in the Evans family.

At around nine years old I'd come through physical therapy and was back performing almost every weekend. My parents thought it was time to get someone with more experience to help refine us and put more professional shows together. So they hired a manager for us. I have no idea where they found him or how. He was just an average guitar player, and I think he could sing a little, but what he didn't have in talent, he made up for in BS. He really took over and I guess he convinced my parents that he knew better than them. None of us liked him; he was a slave driver and also kind of a pervert.

My brothers and I drove from Missouri to Nashville with him one time (just the three of us), and I was probably around ten years old, Matt thirteen, and Jay fifteen. I guess the trip was to try to get some meetings with some bigwigs in Nashville and see if anyone would be interested in signing us. Well, on the way, we stopped at a motel for the night, and he told my brothers to go to the lobby to find snacks. While they were gone, he told me to get in the bed with him and he said, "Give me a goodnight kiss," and he pulled me to his mouth and gave me a very long and very disgusting kiss straight on my lips. I knew instinctively that this was so wrong, and luckily my brothers came back to the room right after that. I jumped up and crawled in bed with them and slept between them so I wouldn't have to be anywhere near the pig. From that point on I never liked him, even though he was our "manager" for several years. I never wanted to be alone with him.

My sisters used to get up on stage and sing "How Much Is That Doggie in the Window" for a special moment in our shows, and he would always come up behind them and grab their bottoms. He was definitely pervy. But when you're a kid you don't feel like you have the power or the authority to question adults in your life. So we just went along with it. Years later I told my mom about the kiss. She was appalled and wished I had told her sooner. It's so sad and scary to me how often this kind of stuff happens to kids and they don't tell anyone. I know for me I felt ashamed and scared and embarrassed. Now as a mom, I would kill anyone who harmed my children, and I would hope they would tell me anything. I think that's something parents should definitely start talking to their kids about from an early age.

Performing is always hard work, and we were staying out till all hours. Our typical bar gigs ran from 9:00 p.m. to 1:00 a.m. on Friday

Me, Lesley, Matt, Jay, and Ashley

and Saturday nights. We played a first set from 9:00 to 9:45 p.m., and then we'd take a fifteen-minute break and start a new set. The night was cut into four sets like that.

One such night, we were starting our second set when I realized I needed to use the bathroom. But it was too late. It was time to start the show again.

Matt was behind me to my left, playing bass, where he still stands to this day every show. I turned and caught Matt's eye. He gave me a questioning look like, "What's wrong?"

I mouthed to him, "I have to pee!"

He squinted, not understanding, so I said it again. His eyes grew large.

"No!" Matt said, and his head snapped toward our manager, who was playing guitar on the other side of the stage. We both knew he would be furious if I left the stage right then, so I grabbed the microphone and started singing, trying to force myself not to think about it. But how could I last for forty-five minutes?

My heart raced. I couldn't remember ever needing to go to the bathroom more than this moment. I didn't think I could hold it till the break. Then I'd try getting through another song.

Finally, it was too much. I couldn't hold it any longer. The band was playing. I kept singing, but I stopped swaying, and right there, I peed on stage!

Thank God I was wearing a skirt and boots, because no one could tell. The pee went straight into my cowboy boots. Nobody even noticed.

I turned to Matt with a horrified expression and mouthed, "I'm peeing!!!!!!!"

"What?!" He'd understood me but was understandably in shock. His eyes were wide as he looked toward my feet and then back at me, and my face surely told the story. However, with our natural talent and hours of practice, we hadn't missed a beat.

It was the longest set of my life. Finally, we played the last song, and I hurried as fast as my sloshing boots would move to the women's bathroom. I still couldn't believe that I had peed on stage—and no one had noticed! I washed up until my boots and legs were dry enough to go back out.

"Hey, Sara!" It was our manager up on stage on his knees, cleaning up a large wet spot. I stopped cold, fearing that everyone, and worst of all our horrible manager, knew my awful secret.

"Watch out up here. Matt spilled an entire pitcher of water on stage. Can you believe that?"

He shook his head in disgust as Matt brought some rags he'd gotten from the bar. I realized that my brother had intentionally spilled that pitcher of water to cover it all up. And there was our manager cleaning up!

"You are such a dork!" Matt whispered under his breath when I came on stage. "Why didn't you just go to the bathroom?"

"I couldn't hold it, and I didn't want to get in trouble for leaving!"

Matt just started laughing, but then it was time to start the next set.

We continued to the end, putting on a good show like we always did.

The next morning, we told our parents what happened. Everyone laughed about it, especially about the manager having to clean up my pee when he thought it was just water. Served him right. It was overall a very funny story that I've told a million times, but it was also kind of traumatizing. I mean, I was just a little girl, and I had no one there to help me clean myself up or take me to the bathroom, or to tell our bully of a manager to let me go to the bathroom anytime I wanted. I think that whole experience really reinforced the idea that I had to be a people pleaser at all times, and never let anyone down. That idea would have more significant ramifications further on in my career.

Chapter 4

DREAMS BROKEN, DREAMS REBORN

It was the 1960s in small-town America. If you didn't go to college, you got married right out of high school, which was exactly what my parents and most of their friends did.

My parents grew up in New Franklin. My dad, Jack (Jackie) Ray Evans, was the third oldest of four children. He was raised by Minnie and Albert Evans (Grandma and Grandpa). Grandpa Evans was a farmer, and Grandma was a school cafeteria cook.

My dad was gorgeous when he was young, with big brown eyes, olive skin, and black hair. He loved leather jackets—and motorcycles and cars and airplanes: anything that went fast. He was the apple of my grandma's eye, and she definitely favored him. He could sing, and he was smart and funny, a great catch for a raven-haired beauty like my mom.

Patricia Ann Floyd, my mom, was the middle child between two brothers; her parents were Mildred and Ralph Floyd, aka Granny and Papa. My mom was a strong and vibrant athlete in high school. She was super-smart, with a wicked sense of humor, and so striking that she looked like a 1960s movie star. Both of my parents could've made it on the big screen, but they chose the simple, small-town life, and right after marriage they started having babies. I think that's just what most people did in the sixties and before.

A year after the wedding, in 1966, my brother Jay was born. My brother Matt followed in 1968. Three years after him, I made my entrance into the world, and Lesley and Ashley followed.

My parents were married for eighteen years before they divorced. When you get married at a young age, it's probably impossible to know who you really are and what you really want out of life. I think that's the story of my parents, to put it simply.

My mom wanted to be a farmer and have a big family. My dad wanted to be a delinquent on *Welcome Back, Kotter* and had dreams of being on the open road with the wind in his face. I inherited my dad's wanderlust, for sure, because I've spent much of my life on the road. I even recorded a song on that topic, called "Restless," which was the title track on my fourth album.

I'm sure my parents didn't marry thinking they'd get a divorce. No one does. But this was the eighties, when divorce wasn't as frowned upon as it had been previously. My parents had a lot of stress with five kids, money problems, multiple jobs, a four-hundred-acre farm, and very different dreams. I can only imagine the many issues that eventually pulled them apart.

It's not that my parents fought. Actually, our family had a lot of fun. I always thought of us as a really cool, tight family, which made it even worse when, during the summer of 1983, my mother told us that my dad had moved out. It was the summer before I started sixth grade.

∞

My parents' divorce was different from most, I think. Like I said, they really didn't fight, but we could see the tension a lot. Especially in those six months before we were told that my dad had moved out. And that's exactly what happened. One Sunday morning we all came downstairs, my mother was cooking breakfast, the little girls were playing in another room, and she told Jay and Matt and me to sit down. She said, "Your dad has moved into an apartment in Columbia so he can be closer to work when he has to do the graveyard shift." I think we all three knew in our hearts that's not why he got an apartment in Columbia. We were too afraid to ask the question, "Are you guys getting a divorce?" But we knew. We all looked at each other, and we knew. And I think it was maybe later that day or not long after when he came home, and we watched them through the window. They were arguing by the car. We were never really told anything more.

One night I was in bed upstairs and the phone rang. We had one phone upstairs and one downstairs. I picked it up as quietly as I could and started listening to my parents' private conversation. I knew it was wrong and I could get into BIG trouble if I got caught, but I couldn't stop! I had to know something about why they were divorcing. All I heard was a bit of a conversation that I didn't really understand before I hung up. I put the phone back on the handle as slowly and quietly as I could and tiptoed back to my bed. That was the first time I cried about everything. I cried and cried, sobbing into my pillow until I fell asleep. So to this day I really can't give you a concrete answer as to why they split.

It wasn't like today's divorces. There weren't any court battles or custody issues, and we never really got into the routine of "every other weekend at Dad's house." It's almost as though we went on with life and Dad didn't live with us anymore.

I remember once or twice we did stay with Dad in his apartment in Columbia. But it was just a one-bedroom apartment, way too small for five kids, and it wasn't fun. In fact, it was kind of depressing. I think he tried to make it fun. He got a bunch of snacks and soda and a little bumper pool table, and our mom let us take the ColecoVision from our house. We tried to make the best of it, but there was no room, it was in a bad part of town, and we had to sleep on the floor, which had dirty wall-to-wall carpeting. We stayed Friday and Saturday night.

On Sunday morning I woke up with the loudest, most horrific noise in my ear! I mean, it was excruciating, and I had absolutely no idea what was happening. I started screaming and crying and panicking, so Dad took me and all five of us to a clinic down the road. They saw me immediately because I was so freaked out from that awful loud noise. Turns out, a teeny-tiny bug had crawled in my ear while I slept on that disgusting carpet. So the doctor poured some kind of fluid (maybe just water, I don't know) in my ear and told me to keep my head tilted for about ten minutes to keep the fluid in, and then he said, "All right, turn your head the other way." And a bug fell out onto a tissue that he was holding. It was so tiny you could barely even see it! I remember being shocked at the loud noise that tiny little bug made and being so relieved that the noise stopped. Just like that. The doc said it was because the bug was lying right on my eardrum. I told you, I am accident-prone. If it's going to happen, it's going to happen to me.

I think we may have only spent one other weekend, if that, at my dad's sad little apartment, and then we began visiting him on Wednesday nights at Grandma and Grandpa Evans's house in New Franklin. Our hometown. But that was kind of terrible, too, because my dad was so depressed. He couldn't even pretend. He would just sit there on the couch and watch TV while we waited until the "visit" was up and we needed to go home to get our homework done or whatever. It was very uncomfortable, and I remember being sick with worry and pity for him. For all of us.

And of course it wasn't too long before the "newness" of the divorce wore off and my dad couldn't make the child support payments. He was struggling big-time financially. I don't know the details or the ins and outs of what agreements or arrangements they made, but I remember Mom saying, "Tell your dad I need the child support." Of course, that is not what any child wants to do. So we would get in the silver van that had become Jay's when he turned sixteen, and discuss this on the way to go see Dad. "What should we say?" "Should we say anything, or just ignore it?" "Will Mom get mad if we don't tell him she needs her check?"

Around this time, Jay, Matt, Lesley, Ashley, and I vowed that we'd always be close and not ever let anything come between us or get in the way of our love for one another. When you're a child of divorce, it's something that you share with your siblings that nobody else can really understand. There's a closeness with all of us that remains to this day.

Everyone, including our extended family, was devastated about my parents' divorce. And in a small town in the eighties, it was embarrassing to say that your parents weren't together. As a family, we had been popular and well known in our town. Everything about it sucked.

∞

Two years after the divorce, my mom married another farmer, my stepfather, Melvin. Mom and Melvin are still married today, and they had two more little girls, my half sisters, Erin and Allyx.

I was fourteen when Erin was born, and much of the responsibility for her care fell on me. In a way, she felt like my own child. Mom had been driving the school bus for many years, so in the mornings, I'd be responsible for watching my baby sister while I got ready for junior high. Then Matt and I would take Erin to school with us, where we'd meet Mom, who'd just finished the bus route. She would take Erin and drive our car home. After school, it was the opposite routine, unless we had sports or a gig to play. Mom would meet us as school was getting out, and we'd take the baby home, where I'd watch her till Mom got done driving the school bus.

Mom and Melvin sold the big farm and moved into another house—this one white—in New Franklin, on forty acres. We packed up the last of our childhood and the family we'd been, saying goodbye to the place we'd loved since I was four years old.

We started growing tobacco at the new farm. My brothers and I were expected to help, as usual, and if I'd thought we'd worked hard before, I soon discovered that tobacco farming was incredibly demanding. Since tobacco is grown year-round, we didn't have the usual seasons of planting, growing, harvesting, and a winter rest in the fields, like we'd had at our old farm. There was a cycle of growing the tobacco, but it didn't stop in winter. Unlike most other crops, every tobacco plant has to be physically handled. Harvesting meant cutting and spearing each of the tall tobacco plants, which were over six feet, and hanging them to dry. During the harvest, we'd get out of school and head straight to the tobacco fields.

There was at least one key benefit to this hard work, and that was the hiring of cute teenage boys to help with the harvest. I was in my early teens and loved being able to put on some short cutoff jean shorts and flirt with them! All of my girlfriends suddenly wanted to help in the tobacco fields, too! The guys were impressed that I was out there, and I put in extra effort showing off that I could work as hard as anyone else.

We still had other work on the farm besides the tobacco. We'd haul hay for the horses and livestock, and do the chores a farm requires. I remember countless times that we'd earn extra money picking up hundreds of bales of hay from someone's pasture. My mom would drive the truck and flatbed trailer and the boys and I would buck every single bale. I would wear shorts because it was so bloody hot, and I'd tie a bandanna around my right leg, the one I used to push the hay bale up onto the trailer. You had to wear work gloves, too, or your hands would get torn up. And, of course, being the competitive tomboy that I was, I HAD to try to buck as many bales as the boys, and I usually did. Maybe more. I love hard physical labor. Love it. And there is always the random bale that you'll pick up and discover a huge snake coiled up under it, and you would scream and run as fast as you could to get away! Everyone would have a good laugh at that.

Mom balanced everything—even while pregnant at thirty-nine and forty-two, she worked nonstop. I watched her change a flat tire just one week before she gave birth to my sister Erin. I can hardly remember her ever slowing down. She was farmer, homemaker, mom, wife, school bus driver, and, for a while, she took on additional work at a gas station and the post office. Melvin worked for the Highway Department in addition to farming. He was always being called out in the middle of the night when it snowed, to clear the roads and get them ready for people to get to work and school the next morning. We hardly ever had snow days. I still can't believe my mom drove the school bus on those days. I would have been scared to death! But again, she's not afraid of anything. She knew exactly how to handle the icy, hilly roads, how to pump the brakes just right so she wouldn't lose control of the bus. She taught us all how to drive in the snow, too. When Mom worked long hours, Lesley and Ashley and I took on the housework, making the beds, doing laundry and dishes, and cooking some of the meals. We knew the work better be done by the time Mom pulled up to the house. Sometimes we'd procrastinate or get busy with other things, like watching TV, and then we'd hear the car coming up the driveway and spring into action.

I remember us calling out, "Mom! Mom's home!" as my sisters and I looked at one another in terror and raced around finishing up the chores before that door opened. There wasn't a question of what would happen if we didn't get it done. We just *better* get those chores done! So to make it fun, we pretended to have powers like Samantha on *Bewitched*, where she could move at triple speed. It was hilarious! But it worked!

It did not escape our minds, though, that we had sort of moved on from the divorce as if nothing had happened. We were carrying on with life as usual. But it was never quite the same.

Meanwhile, my dad was living his own life without us. Eventually, he started to move on after the divorce, and he began dating. He had a cute girlfriend named Malia who was younger than him, with short blond hair. She was nice, but it was strange seeing my father in a relationship like that, looking at a woman other than my mom with affection. I hated it immediately. I felt like he should want to spend his time with us kids now that he was getting back on his feet. But instead, he was so into Malia. At thirteen years of age, I couldn't understand it.

I still wanted to hang out with my dad and be Daddy's girl. The further he pulled away, the more I tried to get him back. I went shopping with Malia and my dad in St. Louis one time. She took me to Banana Republic, which was the kind of store she liked. I walked through the racks of neatly hung clothing, loving the outfits I saw that were so different from the western shop and Walmart clothes that I was used to. Then I looked at the price and swallowed hard at how expensive it was. This was a world way different from what I'd known. I had a feeling at that time that maybe my dad had no idea who he really was or what he really wanted.

Eventually Dad and Malia broke up. He was alone again and unhappy. Then he started dating a very nice woman named Christine—we called her Chris. Dad was happyish again, but that didn't mean he was available to us kids. He made an announcement shortly after they started dating: "Guess what? Christine and I are getting married."

Even though my mom was remarried, it seemed too soon. There was nothing wrong with Chris. She was nice to us, but Dad had just changed so much. With Mom and Melvin, we were an intact family, and Mom hadn't changed. I was beginning to learn that my dad really didn't like to be alone, and that he was a chameleon: once he met a woman, he changed for her and kept getting swept into her world and her ways.

It seemed there was never a time after my parents' divorce when we really had our dad to ourselves. They say that most men are like this, and that when they get divorced, they don't like to be alone for long. They want to get married again, and quickly. But for me, a wedding meant losing my dad forever.

Christine had a daughter the exact same age as me—my new stepsister, Johnna. She was an only child. Dad moved into Chris's beautiful condo in Columbia. I walked around looking at the feminine touches, thinking how strange that my manly dad lived here now. Johnna's room was perfectly decorated and all her own, without siblings. I had shared a bed with my sisters my whole life. She was obsessed with Princess Diana and had every book about her as well, huge picture books, and an array of Princess Di collectible plates on the wall.

Her clothes were the best brands. She seemed to have it all. Guess Jeans. Limited. Izod. And Banana Republic! They were brands I hardly knew about. I didn't have clothes like that. Johnna was also pretty and skinny, with long hair. She was popular at a big high school in Columbia. I felt suddenly insecure, jealous, and depressed. I thought, there is no way I can compete with this girl for my dad's love and attention. She's too perfect, and I'm a reminder of my mom's and his old life.

He spent most of his time with Chris and Johnna now when he wasn't working, and I suddenly felt I had to compete for his attention and his financial support. I liked Johnna, but I was jealous of her. Not of her condo, or her room, or her clothing—well, maybe a little jealous of those things—but mostly because she had my dad. He began to act more like her father than mine, and the three of them had routines, TV shows, restaurants, and plans that weren't ours. I was a guest in my dad's house.

I was about fifteen now and dating my first boyfriend. A great guy from school with a strong family that was very religious and conservative. He was an athlete, and just a solid guy. During the years that I dated him, his friendship, love, and support totally saved me from myself. With the tumult of emotions running through me, I could've really rebelled and fallen in with the wrong crowd.

My siblings and I were successful in sports and school. We still made music and performed, and Mom was pretty strict. None of us got into serious trouble. But I had a void in my heart, a gaping void that longed to be filled.

My boyfriend came with me to my father and Christine's wedding. I'd been okay with Mom's wedding. Melvin living with us didn't change the steadiness of Mom or our routines at home. But with Dad's new marriage, a vast, dark unknown spread before me. I didn't know what I was going to feel now that he had a new wife and step-daughter.

As a bridesmaid in my dad's wedding, I stood with my jaw clenched, trying to hold back the tears. It kept running through my head that Dad was getting married. I tried not to burst into tears. After the ceremony, my brothers and my younger sisters and I were lined up in the receiving line as we shook people's hands and were told things like, "Congratulations" or "We're so happy for you guys." I tried to smile and say thank you, but it was all I could do not to run out of there. The wedding was like this exclamation point that I had truly lost my father.

I'd had three years of knowing this slow loss after my parents' divorce, but still these markers of that loss were salt in an unhealed wound.

I got in my boyfriend's truck and started sobbing. I literally couldn't stop. It was like everything I had been feeling just hit me all at once. He was truly concerned about me. He pulled over and sat there with me for hours while I cried.

The thing was, Chris and Johnna were really good to me, to all of us. Though my new stepsister was spoiled, in my teenage estima-tion, she didn't act like it. We became friends even with the feelings I couldn't iron out. I knew Chris loved us, too. They weren't the reason Dad acted so differently. He was happy again, but that didn't make him become the father I'd known all my years of growing up. I felt rejected, and he saw none of it. Instead of turning away, I became determined to make him love me more.

The summer before seventh grade, Dad and Chris and Johnna were going on vacation to Maine to visit her family and her home-town. Mom and Melvin were planning a vacation to drive to Colo-rado at the same time. The whole family was supposed to go on this vacation, but I didn't want to go. I wanted to go with my dad and Chris and Johnna. I couldn't stand the fact that she was getting to go on this cool trip with MY dad. So I waited until I got the nerve up and broke the news to my mom that I would rather go with my dad. I could tell that it hurt Mom, even though she didn't show it. But I kept picturing Dad getting even closer to my stepsister, and I just wanted to spend time with him.

It was a pretty fun trip. I remember feeling so out of place with the three of them, and being annoyed at how different my dad acted with them. He was not the same person who had raised me. And like I said, there was nothing wrong with Chris or Johnna. These situations are just tough. Looking back, I see that Johnna was in the same situation with her dad, because he had remarried and she had half- or stepsiblings to compete with when she went to visit him. And I also know that none of it was Johnna's fault. She was a child of divorce, just like I was.

My father and Christine's marriage unfortunately didn't last that long. It's true what they say statistically about second marriages. It's hard enough as it is to be married—and then you bring all the baggage of kids, debt, and angry exes. Often people remarry too soon after divorce, before they've had a chance to properly mourn the death of the first marriage. It's possible to have an amazing second marriage. My husband, Jay, and I have been very lucky—after ten years of marriage, we are still madly in love and are over-the-top attracted to each other. But it hasn't always been easy. We've definitely had our share of issues. I think I tend to try everything in my power to avoid fighting, and I let a lot of things go. I was raised to be old-fashioned and submissive to my husband, and that eliminates a lot of fighting. More on that later . . . stop rolling your eyes, ladies!

Another tragedy for kids of divorce (unless it's a good thing, which it very well could be) is that if you have a stepparent, and that marriage ends in divorce, then you most likely will never see that person again. I think I've seen Chris and Johnna just a couple of times since I was a teenager. I have kept in contact with Johnna through social media. She has a great life and is happily married to her high school sweetheart. I'm happy for her.

As the years went by and we got to be in our late teens, Matt and I were the ones who were the most serious about music. We were completely devoted to it and knew it was our life calling. I personally knew that if I didn't sing, I would die inside. It was the one thing that always gave me confidence, and the stage was and is the place where I am most comfortable.

RIVERBOAT
MUSIC and
TALENT

**SARA EVANS
SHOW**

"The Sara Evans Show"

Up until I was sixteen years old, we always had bands. Usually they consisted of me singing lead, Jay playing acoustic guitar, Matt playing bass, and other local musicians on drums, fiddle, electric guitar, steel guitar, you name it. And we worked almost every single weekend. But when Jay graduated from high school in 1984, he quickly got married and started a family of his own, so he quit music. Matt graduated in 1986 and decided to go to college, so he moved in with Granny and Papa in Columbia and attended Mizzou.

I heard about this huge dance hall that had opened up on the other side of Columbia called the Country Stampede. I called them to see if they'd be interested in hiring me to sing lead in the house band, and they invited me to come audition. They had already heard of me from my work in the area. From the farm it was well over an hour to get there, but that didn't matter to me. I think they paid something like fifty or a hundred dollars a show. The shows were every Saturday night from nine to one, and you had to rehearse on Wednesday nights. I went and sang for the owner, a guy named Mike Glass, who also played guitar in the band, and he hired me on the spot. I was barely sixteen years old and had a piece of crap car called Le Car. Every time I turned the heater on, smoke would start blowing out of every vent and crevice in the dang thing. But I didn't care. I saw the Country Stampede as a stepping-stone that could get me closer to Nashville.

I absolutely loved that job and made some dear friends. There was another female singer named Connie who was probably in her thirties at the time, and her husband was the bass player. And then there was this amazing singer/guitarist named Darren Payne. He had such a cool country voice. He covered all the current male hits and I covered all the current female hits, with Connie singing harmony. And when Darren and I sang duets together, we were fantastic! We were both sixteen and reaching for the stars. He was a really small guy with a huge low voice and could sing anything. His parents idolized him and he drove a huge brand-new truck. When he was twenty years old, he and his wife were driving home from a party and he was hit and killed by a drunk driver. He would have been a huge star. I know it.

It was a fun place to work, but it was truly a job, like singing at Opryland or Dollywood or Disney. We were told what to sing and what to wear and how to dance and everything. It helped my stage presence get better, but I was BORED! After a year or so, I realized that I missed the freedom to choose what songs I wanted to sing and what I wanted to wear, and what musicians I wanted to work with. Plus, I liked other genres of music besides just country. I loved Fleetwood Mac, the Eagles, Belinda Carlisle, REO Speedwagon, Heart, and many, many more groups and musicians. I was itching to put a band together with Matt again and hire our own musicians and start playing clubs and sing whatever I wanted to sing. But my mom loved the fact that I worked at the Country Stampede. I think she felt that I was safe there and it was steady work, and she and Melvin loved to come and watch me perform and dance! I was torn between making my mother happy and doing what I wanted. You know when you're a teenager and your brain isn't fully developed, so you do really stupid things sometimes? Yeah.

Matt and I secretly assembled a band and started practicing and learning songs and putting a four-set show together. It was something we knew how to do really well from years and years of experience. We thought, we can book shows with this band on any night except Saturdays. That will work, right? Well, I don't remember all the details, but somehow someone double-booked us, and we had a show in Mexico, Missouri, on a Saturday night. So I did the dumbest thing I've ever done (and I'm not a liar—I detest lying): I called in sick to the Country Stampede and told them I had strep throat.

Mexico is about a forty-five-minute drive from the Country Stampede. We were in the middle of our show, rockin' along, and I looked up and saw Mike Glass's wife, Sue, standing in the middle of the dance floor in this little hole-in-the-wall bar just staring, no, glaring at me! I almost peed on stage again! I turned around and looked at Matt to make sure he saw her, too. I was praying it was just a figment of my imagination. Well, we knew we were dead meat. Matt was already eighteen, out of the house and in college, but he was just as scared of Mom as I was. Sue stood there for about ten seconds and then did a smooth 180 and marched out of that bar. Before we even finished our show, they called my mom and fired me. I'm not sure if I'm glad there were no cell phones yet or not. On the one hand, I could have texted everyone to say I'm sorry and wouldn't have had to talk to anyone, but on the other hand, there would have been a lot of mean texts waiting for me when I left the stage.

As we packed up our gear, we all talked about how badly we felt about the whole thing and how scared we were. Needless to say, Mom was very disappointed in us, and rightly so. I've never done anything like that since. And I did call the Country Stampede and profusely apologize.

I will never regret starting our own band, though. There was something about that band, with those musicians, that was really special. And the experience helped me grow so much as an artist. I was also developing a crush on the drummer in our band, and I was about to be a senior in high school. My longtime boyfriend and I had broken up. I decided for my senior year I didn't want to be tied down, and he was a year ahead of me, so I didn't want to be jealous that he was at college with a lot of beautiful girls. We had dated for more than two years, and that's a long time for teenagers.

I'm drawn to talent and success. This guy in our band was a great drummer, a natural, and his brother played guitar and sang in the band, too. We started dating, and he even went to my senior prom with me. I thought I was in love with him, but what I didn't realize is that I had developed a warped sense of what being loved was because of how things had turned out with my dad. If a guy was possessive and jealous and wanted me all to himself, I saw that as love: Wow, he doesn't want me to even talk to anyone else—he really, really loves me! If he's nice and normal and shows me affection and doesn't care if I have my own life and friends, then he probably doesn't really love me or is about to choose another girl over me.

If a girl loses her relationship with her dad, or he's absent, she can begin to think like this. I was beginning to develop unhealthy views about men and how men felt about me. I didn't value myself enough to think that I deserved to be treated well. I totally blamed myself for the way I believed my dad thought of me. The drummer was the first of many men I would allow to treat me poorly.

I wanted to be loved in a way I couldn't express or understand. I made excuses for the drummer, blaming myself for making him angry, or for arguing with him. I began "begging" men to love me instead of choosing a man whose love was healthy and normal and genuine, who understood give-and-take and trust. I started telling myself that in order to be loved by a man, I had to say yes to everything he wanted and never do anything to make him mad, and make sure he never liked another girl more than me because he might leave. And I was so tired of being left. After Mom and Dad's divorce, Dad didn't purposefully hurt me, but he ignored me, and that did more damage to me than I realized. It wasn't my dad's fault that I chose to allow someone to abuse me, but he was a part of the reason.

Ladies, a man who has bad intentions and wants to manipulate and abuse women can smell that lack of self-esteem in you and will latch on to you like white on rice. Abusive and narcissistic men can see an insecure and overly submissive woman from miles away, and they know exactly what to say and do to trap you. They will treat you like a queen and shower you with love and attention until they've got you, and then they turn on you like a rabid dog. Be careful, because there are dangerous men everywhere. Be wise and choose a good man. I know women are drawn to the bad-boy image, but you have to make sure that your bad boy isn't abusive, and that your good boy isn't, either. Because they come in all kinds of disguises. I wouldn't start to see through the drummer's disguises for quite some time.

Chapter 5

NASHVILLE CARS

Just a few months before I graduated from high school, my mom had another baby, my youngest sister, Allyx. As much as I adored my baby sisters, I felt ready to leave home, too. I'd turned eighteen and knew that my childhood was behind me now. In many ways, it felt like I'd been an adult for years already.

During my senior year, all my friends were applying to college, and I got swept up in that excitement. I graduated in May of 1989, and in September 1988 Matt had gone to Hollywood to attend MI, Musicians Institute. It's a very prestigious school, at the time focused on jazz. He went there to study bass, which had been his main instrument since he was about nine years old. Our band had broken up, all my friends were going to college, and I thought I should go, too. I had been offered a full scholarship in music at a small private college called Central Methodist University in Fayette, Missouri. My oldest brother, Jay, took me aside one day at Mom's and basically begged me to take it. He was a proud big brother but also concerned for me, and he thought that I should definitely get a college degree so I would have something to fall back on if it didn't work out in Nashville. He also reminded me that I'd be the first Evans kid to pursue an academic degree, and that made me very proud. It was also a lot of pressure. It meant so much to me that he cared about me like that. Being five years older than me, he had already gotten married and started his own family. In a lot of ways he's always been like a father figure to me.

It didn't dawn on me until I actually got to college that I wasn't the college type. Growing up singing in bars and living such a different life than most, I didn't feel like a normal eighteen-year-old girl. We had no money, so I wasn't showing up with new cute clothes and cute dorm stuff. My mom was distracted with the new baby, and Erin was just three and a half, so she wasn't really available to help me. I vaguely remember the day I moved in—it was awful. Everything in my being was screaming, "This isn't right! This isn't for you!" I remember going to some kind of party the first night with my new roommate and just feeling so out of place. Plus I was still in a serious relationship with the drummer at this time, and all I wanted to do was be with him. During the first few days, I started my music theory class, and if you've ever taken music theory, you know how unbelievably hard it is. It's all math, and I'm horrible at math! You know that feeling when you're in class and you don't understand anything and you just want to cry? Also, I had to take a class called Death and Dying, and it TOTALLY freaked me out. It made me start thinking about death when I should have been on cloud nine knowing that I was just starting my life as an adult and I had my whole life ahead of me. I became depressed. Very depressed.

Fayette is only twenty minutes or so from our farm, so I never stayed in the dorm. I went home almost every night. Matt graduated from MI in September, and as soon as he got home, he came to visit me at school. We sat outside on a gorgeous fall day—the kind of day where the air is crisp and the sky is so blue and there's a feeling in the air that makes you think anything is possible—and I sobbed, explaining how miserable I was. And he said the most perfect and simple thing: "Then quit. Sara, you don't have to go to college if you don't want to. Just go talk to the dean and tell him your feelings." I was so worried that everyone would be mad at me for wanting to quit and not take advantage of the full ride I had been given, but Matt gave me the push I needed to leave. I made an appointment to speak to the dean the next day and he completely got it. He said, "Look, college isn't for everyone, and you've got the natural talent to make it big. My advice to you is to go for it." I will always be grateful to him for understanding. The only problem was that since I was quitting, I owed them a little over four hundred dollars. I had absolutely no money, and my mom didn't have an extra four hundred dollars lying around, so I went to the bank in New Franklin. I asked them if I could borrow four hundred dollars, to be paid back over six months, and they loaned it to me. I drove to Central Methodist, handed them the check, went to the dorm, and got my things. And I was out of there!

I think it's extremely important not to settle in life. I see so many people just settling for less than the best because they don't think they deserve the best. Or they are too lazy to try. I believe that anything is possible. Or at least worth a shot. And if you don't reach the ultimate goal that you're setting for yourself, have some alternate plans that you would still be happy with. People are always asking me for advice on how to make it in the music industry. It pretty much always goes like this: "Sara, I love to sing. What advice do you have for someone like me who's trying to break into the business?"

The first thing I always ask is: "Are you willing to sacrifice what others aren't?"

And this is something I've really tried to drive home to my kids their whole lives. "Are you willing to sacrifice what others aren't?" Meaning, if you want to go for something big, something that will pay big, you better be willing to forgo having a girlfriend or boyfriend, partying, sleeping, smoking pot all day and pretending you're being creative, playing Xbox (don't even get me started on Xbox, and thank God my kids never got into it—not that I would have let them play it 24/7), binge-watching TV shows, getting married too young, having kids too young, or a million other things that are fun to do and that most people either find desirable or just fall into. Are you willing to wait? Are you willing to wait for those things and put your dreams first?

I have a theory called the "Open Door Theory." It's nothing brilliant. When you are young, essentially every door in life is open to you, and every time you make a big, life-altering decision before the age of twenty-five or so, you close one of those doors. And that's okay for a lot of people. There are millions of people who get married young and have kids young and work jobs and have very simple lives, and that's GREAT. That's how I grew up. But if you are someone who has dreams of being a musician or an actor or hugely successful in business, or whatever it may be, you have to be willing to keep those doors open for as long as you possibly can.

I had no doubt that I'd made the right decision about college, but as expected, my mom was very disappointed. She thought I was crazy to quit school. I'm sure making it big in Nashville didn't sound like a viable plan or a way to make a living. But she got over it and loved me anyway. Now I had to GET A JOB AND SAVE MONEY. I ended up getting hired at a restaurant called Piccadilly's at the Holiday Inn in

Columbia. I was living at home and driving forty-five minutes every morning to wait tables on the 7:00 a.m.–3:00 p.m. shift. I absolutely loved that job. I loved waiting tables! I think everyone should wait tables at least once in their life. Ellen DeGeneres said that on her Netflix special, and I totally agree with her. Waiting tables is so hard. People can be rude and demanding, and they have no idea what a waiter might be going through. You're usually dealing with mean cooks and you have to remember so much and handle so many things at once. You also have to do a lot of the food preparation. For example, many restaurants require the waiters to make the dinner salads, on top of everything they're doing. But I love hard work with a good amount of stress and chaos thrown in at all times. I also became best friends with the manager of the restaurant, Celia. She is fifteen years older than me, and she instantly took me under her wing. She was the first of many connections I would eventually have with Alabama. She was from a small town called Ozark and had somehow made her way up to Missouri and was married to a farmer. They lived outside the city limits. She thought I did such a good job as a waitress that she promoted me to shift manager. So I got to dress up and sit at the front counter and seat people as they came in. When four people needed to be seated, I would tell a waiter that they "had a four top." I also ran the register and had to count the money at the end of every shift.

Celia was having her first child around this time, so a lot of responsibility fell on me, and I thrived in that situation. She was like the big sister I never had. She had so much wisdom and she was a great cook and just full of grace and elegance. Also, she was not a fan of the drummer. I used to take trips with her to Ozark for a week or two in the summers, and I absolutely loved her hometown, her house, her family, her parents, everything. They were the epitome of the South. Her mom was an amazing cook and made me things that I had not grown up eating, like fried okra, fried green tomatoes, and boiled peanuts. Celia was the youngest of four kids, and the only girl. I adored her older brothers and they adored me. They were a good seventeen to twenty years older than me, and I had a huge crush on her oldest brother. Plus, they were all into music and played guitar. One brother even played steel guitar. They belonged to the country club, and we would go there to play tennis—her brothers taught me how to play. I loved everything about going to visit Ozark with Celia.

Shortly after I started working at Piccadilly's, I got an apartment with a friend in Columbia. The drummer had gotten a gig with another very popular band that played big shows all over Missouri and the surrounding states, and he had a place that he shared with his bandmates. We were spending a ton of time together, and I think he was really hoping that I would settle down, forget my dreams, marry him, and watch him play drums. Not a chance. You see, even though I was too submissive and allowed myself to be abused, my drive to become a famous country singer was stronger than that. Than anything. I was getting closer and closer to my goal of moving to Nashville with Matt. We had saved almost a thousand dollars each, which was our goal, and we were almost ready to move. I was almost ready to leave the drummer.

Then something happened that rocked my world again. My dad called one day to see if he could stop by my apartment because he needed to talk to me. We decided that he would pick me up and we would go to lunch. The call made me nervous, because I wasn't used to my dad reaching out to me like that. As I was throwing my jacket on, I heard his horn beep. I ran outside and jumped in his car and said, "Ready to go?" And he said, "No, I actually want to tell you something before we go." So we sat there in the parking lot with his car running and he told me that he had gotten a great job offer in Dallas . . .

I couldn't believe what I was hearing. Dallas? But that's . . . so . . . far . . . from Missouri. I was also upset because he and Chris had been divorced for a little while, and I had envisioned Dad and me getting a lot closer now that he was on his own again. He would have a lot more time to hang out because he was single. But now he was telling me that was not to be the case. He assured me that he would come back to visit all the time and he would fly me there to visit him, but I was doubtful that was going to happen. I was visibly upset and asked him if he was sure about the move, but he just said he couldn't pass it up. The money was too good to turn down. And he said, "Hey, you're moving to Nashville soon anyway, so what's the difference?"

I knew that was a good point, but Missouri was our base. Lesley and Ashley were still minors, living at home. How would they feel when he told them? I knew that anytime I came home from Nashville to visit for holidays or whatever, he wouldn't be there. He would be in Dallas. I told him that I didn't really feel like going to lunch anymore

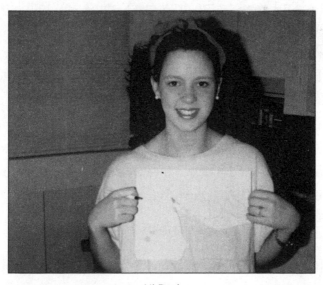

Hi Dad

and that I was tired and maybe we could go another time. I was mad. I was hurt. I was so sad.

This news made me cling to the drummer even more. I felt like I was being abandoned, and I wanted comfort and love. I think he saw this as his perfect chance, and shortly after my meeting with Dad, he started talking about our relationship and our future. "Maybe we should move in together. Heck, let's just get married," he said. A proposal!

I went home to tell Mom. When I pulled up, she was working in the tobacco beds. Immediately I bent down to start helping her pull plants, and I said that the drummer wanted me to marry him. "And I'm considering it," I added. Well, you would have thought I'd said I was shaving my head and moving to Mars! She flipped out. I had no idea how much she didn't like the drummer. Not only that, but I had no idea how supportive my mom really was of my dream to move to Nashville and make it big. We got into a big HUGE fight, and I'd never felt so loved.

That night I went to the drummer's house and told him that it wasn't even an option for me to think about getting married. It did not go over well. At . . . all. He and I tried to make it work for a little longer, but he became more and more volatile, and I knew it was about time for me to get the hell out of Dodge.

So Matt and I packed up Mom and Melvin's two-ton pickup truck, and along with Mom and my best friend, Stefi, we headed to Music City, USA! We looked like the Beverly Hillbillies. Mom drove the truck, and Matt and I each drove our cars.

∞

Let me tell you about Stefi. She is one of those friends you make when you're in elementary school and you just know the moment you meet that you're soul mates. We were almost never apart until we graduated from high school. We did everything together. We were always at one or the other's houses, and we never got tired of each other. There were times in my childhood when I don't know what I would have done without her. We are opposites as far as looks. She is short, with blond hair, and I am tall, with black hair. But we were twins in every other way. And talk about funny. She is funny, and you have to be funny to be my friend or to be a part of my family. When she turned sixteen, three months before me, her parents bought her a Cadillac. We thought we were so cool. All we did was drive around in that car and listen to REO Speedwagon, the Eagles, and the Charlie Daniels Band. We were inseparable. She was maid of honor in my first wedding and I was maid of honor in hers.

Stefi had a sister named Kim who was two years older than us, and when Stefi and I were twenty-eight, Kim was diagnosed with cancer. She had just had a baby and was having trouble with her digestive system, which is normal post-pregnancy, but it wouldn't get any better. She went to specialists and they discovered that she had rectal cancer. Her ob-gyn missed a tumor that was there at a routine post-delivery exam. That was around Thanksgiving of 2001, about a year and three months after Avery was born.

Kim and Stefi called me together to tell me, and I said, "I'm going to start praying, and you're going to be fine. You can beat this, and I am here for you, whatever you need!" And all the other comforting things I could possibly think of to say. But when I hung up the phone I had a dark, dark feeling. She started treatment and I just kept praying—my entire hometown was praying—but my mom would call and tell me that she had seen Kim at a ballgame or whatever and that she did not look good. The following August, I went on the Girls' Night Out Tour with Reba McEntire, Martina McBride, Jamie

O'Neal, and Carolyn Dawn Johnson. Reba was headlining, of course. Our first show was set to be in Vegas, and they wanted us to be there two days early so we could rehearse a big encore where all of us would come out at the end of Reba's set and sing with her.

On the first day of rehearsal, my cell phone rang. I was putting Avery to bed in his crib in the hotel suite and waiting for the nanny to come to the room so I could go to rehearsal. Seeing Stefi's name on the caller ID gave me the worst feeling in the world. I didn't want to answer, because I was afraid of the news that was waiting for me on the other end of the line. Stefi said, "Hey, bitty"—which is what we have called each other since high school—"it's not good news. She's really failing fast, and I think we need to prepare ourselves for the worst." I asked if I could speak to her and I did for just a few minutes. I asked her if she had accepted Jesus into her heart, and she said that she had, and I told her that she would be in heaven with Him and never be sick again and that I loved her so much.

My nanny came in, and I left with my tour manager, who was waiting outside my hotel room door to escort me. He texted ahead and told Reba's people what was going on, and Reba came straight up to me and gave me the biggest hug. She's a class act. The next morning, Kim passed away. The timing was very fortunate, because we had those days off. Matt and I jumped on a plane and flew home for the funeral.

I gave the eulogy and sang "Amazing Grace." At the gravesite, I also sang "One More Day," originally sung by Diamond Rio. It was so horrible and sad. But I was glad that Matt and I were able to leave the tour for a few days to be with Stefi and her family. In 2019, Stefi's son-in-law was killed. Her daughter Abbey had married a professional bull rider, Mason Lowe, ranked number eighteen in the world. He died tragically after being stepped on by a bull that had just thrown him off. I woke up the morning after the accident to about fifty text messages from friends and family asking me if I'd seen the news about Mason. My heart just sank. I immediately called Stefi, and she asked if my sisters and I would sing for the funeral. Of course we said yes. Mason was only twenty-five, leaving behind a twenty-three-year-old widow. Even though the circumstances of the visit were awful, it was really great to get to see my sweet childhood best friend. We always fall right back into the rhythm of our friendship. It's such a blessing to have friends.

∞

Stefi drove down to Nashville with me in my car, and helped Matt and me get settled into our first place, on Briley Parkway. It was a crappy two-bedroom apartment in a not great part of town, but we didn't care—it was OURS, and our only thought was: "Let the games begin!"

Chapter 6

DISCOVERIES

I knew that I was going to need a job as soon as I arrived in Nashville, so Celia helped me get hired at the Holiday Inn, also on Briley Parkway. I waited tables for the breakfast shift. The drummer and I were finished by this time, and I was a single, vulnerable young woman again. One day I met one of the room service waiters and we started dating. I thought that I could handle dating and focusing on my music, but before long I was spending all my time with him. I could see that it was beginning to fracture my relationship with Matt.

On top of everything else, Papa Floyd passed away in November of 1991. That just about did us in, because we were so close to him. Grandpa Evans had also passed away shortly before we moved to Nashville. We were just as close to him. We had to make the eight-hour drive home for Papa's funeral, and when we got back to Nashville, I could tell that something was going on with my brother. He seemed upset with me for having a boyfriend and being distracted (and rightly so), but I could tell he was distracted by something else. What I didn't know was that after my dad's divorce from Chris, his older sister, my Aunt Sharon, had been talking to him about joining her religion. She and her family had been in that organization for years. My dad had been going to their meetings and continued to do so after he moved to Dallas. Then one day after Papa's funeral, Matt told me that he was thinking about moving to Dallas and was curious about my dad's new religion. He just wasn't really sure what he believed, so he was exploring. I think the more he and Dad talked about it, the more Matt really wanted to go all-in. While I was being an idiot and spending all my time with the waiter, Matt indeed left Nashville and moved to Dallas to live with my dad.

I was devastated. But looking back, I totally understand it. I blew it. If you really want to do something big with your life, especially in the entertainment world, you have to be willing to sacrifice what others won't. Like dating the waiter. But at the time I blamed Matt, and I felt like he was abandoning me, and I REALLY hated my dad for influencing him. Matt was my best friend, a twin-like brother who had been playing bass and singing with me since I was four years old. But I let him down when I prioritized my romance with the waiter. When he went to visit Dad in Texas and decided to stay, I had no idea that it would take seven years before we were back together in a band. In that time, my life would change completely.

The waiter and I continued to date. He was in Nashville with two of his brothers and a friend, trying to pursue music as well. They had a band that was kind of an Eagles meets Creedence Clearwater Revival sound. They were all living in a rented duplex near where Matt and I were living. I had a great time hanging out with him and his brothers and just having fun. They are from Oregon, and not long after we started dating, he told me that they were planning to spend the summer out west, doing shows that they had booked. He wanted to know if I wanted to take a road trip and go out there with them for the summer. I thought that sounded like so much fun. So in May of 1992 I packed up my car and we drove across the country. I think we were a caravan of three vehicles. We listened to music and camped on the way to save money. One night I'll never forget, we stopped in the desert. We set up camp, went to town and got supplies, including lots of beer, and camped with a billion stars all around. We listened to "Peaceful Easy Feeling" by the Eagles over and over again. I was twenty-one and he was twenty-nine, and I was drawn to the fact that he was in music, came from a family of seven kids, like me, and grew up on a farm. Most important, because he was eight years older than me, I thought he would take care of me.

I was excited to arrive in Oregon and meet his two younger sisters and two older brothers. The day we arrived, his youngest sister, who was sixteen at the time, was skipping school and lying out on the roof of their house trying to get her tan started for the summer. I thought she was hilarious and just adorable. In fact, I instantly liked everyone in his family, but his mother did NOT like me. She didn't know anything about me except that I was not from Oregon, and that meant I might convince her beloved son to live somewhere other than close to home. I thought that was strange, since he was already living far from home in Nashville. I thought once she got to know me she would love me—even though I knew that our ultimate plan was to return to Nashville.

That summer, I accompanied him and his band all over the Willamette Valley and sat in the audience while they performed their four-hour sets. It was NOT easy for me to be a band girlfriend, because I was so used to being on stage, and the waiters soon recognized that and started asking me to get up and sing with them. The crowds went wild, and I started doing more and more singing, until I became a permanent member of the band. I think this caused the rest of the band to resent me a little, but they couldn't deny the attention we were getting.

Then it dawned on me—we weren't making plans to go back to Nashville. We were booking more shows. I could tell that he was not in any hurry to leave Oregon. I started pestering him about it, and then out of the blue, with no warning and no ring, he asked me to marry him. I said yes. I know. I know what you're thinking . . .

He convinced me that we needed to get jobs and start saving money for the wedding (which I insisted would be in Missouri, in my hometown), and then after we got married, we would move back to Nashville. All in all, we spent three years in Oregon before we finally moved back. I basically told him that I was going and he could come with me or not. I was NOT going to let go of my dream.

Sometime before Matt and I moved to Nashville, before I met the waiter, we met this guy from the Ozarks in Missouri who was a millionaire, and someone told us that we should try to get him to invest in us and our careers. He agreed to sign a three-year contract with us—we'd write songs, and he would pay us each four hundred dollars a month. He had a lawyer in Nashville who told us that we, too, needed a lawyer to protect us in this deal. He suggested that we go see a woman named Brenner Lackey. She was an attorney who practiced music business law. Matt and I immediately loved her. You know when you meet someone and you instantly connect? That was us with Brenner. She helped us negotiate the contract with the millionaire, and then we didn't see her again until the waiter and I returned to Nashville. During the time we were in Oregon, the millionaire paid for me to go into a studio in Portland and record three or four songs to have as a demo to play for people when I got back to Nashville.

Once back in Music City, I knew that one of the first things I should do was meet up with Brenner to make sure I was all clear of that old contract. She was so excited to hear that I had moved back. I played her my demo and she flipped out. She loved my voice. She also told me that she, too, had recently gotten married, and that her husband was a song plugger. That is a person who works for the big music publishing companies and it's their job to get clients' songs recorded by major artists. When a writer completes a song, the publisher hires a great unsigned singer to go into the studio with a band and make a recording of the song. This is called being a "demo singer." Then the song plugger pitches the song to the record labels in hopes that one of their artists will record it. Brenner's husband immediately started getting me work as a demo singer. And I hired Brenner to be my manager.

It wasn't long before word traveled around town. People were saying things like, "Have you heard that new girl Sara Evans?" and "She's got the 'countryist' voice that I've heard in years," and "She's the real deal."

Soon I built up a reputation on Music Row as the new cool singer in town. This led to an opportunity to cover a Harlan Howard song, "I've Got a Tiger by the Tail." Buck Owens co-wrote and had turned that song into a hit back in 1965. Harlan's publisher wanted Patty Loveless to remake the song, so they hired me to sing the demo. Since Patty Loveless had been one of my idols for years, I knew how to make my voice sound just like hers.

When I walked out of the singing booth, I saw an older man sitting on a couch. I was stunned when I recognized that it was Harlan

Howard himself. The man was a legend. He'd written thousands of songs and would eventually be inducted into the Country Music Hall of Fame.

"Hey there, little gal. My God, you sound so good!" he said, rising from the couch. "You remind me of Loretta Lynn when she moved to town. I'm Harlan Howard."

"Yes, sir, I know who you are. I'm honored to meet you," I said, shaking his hand. "And I'm so glad I didn't know you were out here until I was done."

He laughed, then said, "I'm gonna call my friend Renee Bell and tell her that she has to meet you."

Renee Bell was the head of A&R (Artists & Repertoire) for RCA Records. She was the person who found new artists for the label, helped the artists find songs, and then hooked them up with cowriters. In general, she developed a new artist's identity. Renee Bell was

The legendary Harlan Howard

a power person in Nashville, so to have a lunch meeting with her was a BIG deal.

Brenner and I started brainstorming about what I should say to Renee, and what I should wear. But at this time I had no money and no style, so I chose basic black. The three of us met at the Pancake Pantry in Hillsboro Village on my twenty-fourth birthday. Renee and I immediately hit it off.

"I really like you, everything about you, your look, your personality, and I already know you have an amazing voice," Renee said at the end of the meeting. "I want you to come in and sing for Joe next week." Joe was Joe Galante, THE top guy at RCA Records. Everyone in the Nashville music scene knew of him. He had the instinct and the power to take a young talent and turn him or her into a star. He had recently returned to RCA Nashville after being at RCA in New York. He'd signed people like Waylon Jennings, Dolly Parton, the Judds, Clint Black, Vince Gill, Kenny Chesney, Brad Paisley, and Martina McBride. I couldn't believe that I was going to sing for him! I didn't sleep for a week in anticipation. I still had no style and no money, so I took out a credit card at Express in the Green Hills Mall so I could buy an outfit for my big audition.

I decided to sing three songs for Joe. One was a beautiful blue-grassy waltz called "When the Last Curtain Falls"; another was a sad song called "One Girl Cried." And there was one more that I can't remember the name of. I was as ready as I could be. When we pulled up for the meeting at the RCA building, we saw a man getting out of a limo ahead of us, and Brenner said, "Oh my gosh, that's Joe right there."

At the sight of Joe Galante walking into the building, I suddenly became overwhelmed with the magnitude of what I was about to do and how it could change my life. We waited a few minutes so we wouldn't run into him in the hallway, because how awkward would that have been? We took the elevator up to the fourth floor, where a receptionist was waiting for us. Brenner walked up and said, "We have Sara Evans here to see Joe Galante."

The receptionist told us to take a seat, and that Joe would see us in a moment. I was literally sweating, even though it was February.

"Joe is ready for you," the receptionist said, and led us to a small listening room. Joe had a welcoming smile and friendly blue eyes.

We introduced ourselves, and Joe said, "Well, are you ready to sing?"

I suddenly felt so much gratitude to my mom for putting me on stage when I was four years old, because my instincts as a performer took over.

This was my shot. I took a breath, opened my mouth, and sang my heart out. I caught Renee smiling at Joe as if to say, *I told you.* Joe grinned back. While I was singing "One Girl Cried," I actually saw tears in Joe's eyes, and I knew that I was moving him. I sang my very best in that little room. When I finished, I knew I had killed it. We visited for a few more minutes, and Joe had a big smile on his face the whole time.

"Thank you for coming in," he said, and then he looked at Brenner. "I'll give you a call."

We decided to go to Brenner's house and open a bottle of wine and wait. By the time we reached her house, there was already a message on her answering machine. She pushed the button, and we heard Joe's voice. "Brenner, this is Joe Galante. I love Sara!" He pronounced it *Saaaa-ra*, with a thick New York accent. I loved the way Joe said my name for the next eighteen years.

Brenner and I looked at each other. Then we heard Joe's stunning next words, "I would like to offer her a seven-album deal."

I'm sure there were more details to that message, but after I heard "seven-album deal," all I did was scream for the next thirty minutes. Later I heard this was one of the biggest deals anyone had signed in Nashville, maybe ever. And even if it wasn't, it felt that way to me! We literally could not believe it.

And just like that, my career took off.

∞

Everything changed after that. Right away, I quit my job and we hired one of the best music attorneys out of LA, a guy named Gary Gilbert. After several weeks of back-and-forth negotiations, my deal was ready. The label arranged a press conference and had all of the media outlets present when I signed that seven-album deal. With the signing advance from the label, I thought I was rich. I was on cloud nine.

I decided to have Pete Anderson produce my first album. He was Dwight Yoakam's producer and guitar player, and together they created a unique sound that was so musically cool to me. It was West Coast hillbilly country, and I loved it!

We packed up and moved to LA after a few months of cowriting and gathering songs with Renee Bell's help. The album turned out awesome—we all felt it. It bordered on hillbilly country, had a Patsy Clinesque vibe and featured a song I cowrote with Aimee Mayo and Ron Harbin called "Three Chords and the Truth." That was also the title of the album. It came from a famous quote by Harlan Howard, who said a great country song is made up of "three chords and the truth."

We felt like we had gold in our hands.

However, what I'd soon find out was that the hardest part of the music industry wasn't getting a record deal, like I'd always believed. I quickly learned that for country singers, getting the deal was the easy part. Getting played on country radio was much, much harder. At that time, you couldn't become famous without being heard on the radio, and believe me, the program directors never let you forget that fact. It's different today, with the Internet and Spotify, Apple Music, and Pandora, etc. In 1997, country radio was the only mainstream outlet to get your music heard.

After the album was finished, we set about getting it played on country radio. The process started with a radio tour, during which I traveled with a promotion staff from the label by bus, private jet, or rental car to nearly every radio station in America. While there, I played my new music, introduced myself on air, went to dinner with the station executives or took them to lunch, performed free shows, and really did almost anything they wanted in exchange for spins on their station. It was very much like a political campaign, and I came to realize that country radio held all the power in determining the success of my career.

For all of my years of working hard on the farm or performing late into the night at honky-tonk bars while still in school, I never knew what being tired was until I went on a radio tour. It's a different tired from working hard on a farm. On a radio tour, I had to perform, keep a big smile on my face, be ready to laugh and joke and share my music, and always be *on*.

At the end of the radio tour, we found out that even though my album had garnered tons of critical acclaim, country radio didn't like *Three Chords and the Truth*. They flat-out refused to play it, saying it was too country.

Talk about bursting your bubble. After doing all of that work, being so proud of the music, excited about my career launching, I wasn't getting air play. It was the most disheartening experience of my life—at least at that point.

I think I actually heard a *"wah wah wah."*

But if my life had taught me anything at that point, it was to never quit, especially on my music. I knew it was my calling, and being born an optimist, I've never stayed down for long. That's one of the great lessons that getting hit by a car taught me. I knew God had a purpose for me. That's why he had saved me from death. So there was no way in hell I was going to let country radio beat me. I made a plan to go back and perfect what I would give country radio and force them to play me. I knew I had a partner even bigger than Joe Galante behind me.

Chapter 7

JESUS LOVES ME, THIS I KNOW

I am not a fan of organized religion.

I *am* a follower of Jesus Christ, and I believe every word of the Bible to be true. But I have never thought that any man or group should come between me and my relationship with the Lord, and all too often that's the case in organized religion.

I grew up going almost every Sunday to a little white country church called Boonesboro Christian Church. Every week, the service was the same. We'd sing hymns, then children were dismissed to Sunday school, the adults would listen to whatever country preacher the congregation could afford (I remember once our preacher was also a lawyer—what an oxymoron!), then the children came back in, we'd sing more hymns, recite the Lord's Prayer, pass the collection plate, sing another hymn, then we'd sing the closing hymn, which was always "God Be with You." We would sing one verse and then say goodbye.

God be with you till we meet again,
by His counsels guide, uphold you
With His sheep securely fold you
God be with you till we meet again.

To the Evans family, religion and God were a Sunday thing. As our family walked out the doors of that church on Sunday afternoon, we pretty much left God inside. At the age of ten, I got baptized because that's what I was expected to do. I tried to live an upright and moral life, as my parents and grandparents taught me. Looking back, I'm glad that our family went to Boonesboro Christian Church, because it did put the Word of God in my heart, and it was the beginning of my foundation. I didn't doubt that God was always with me. My accident had proven that. But I didn't understand what true salvation was until I was twenty-one years old.

∞

I was working as a waitress in Nashville, trying to navigate Music City on my own. My brother Matt was in Dallas, and I felt really lost and alone without him.

I was out of town staying in a hotel. I picked up the Gideon Bible and just decided to start reading. When I got back to Nashville, I bought my own Bible and read it front to back. I couldn't put it down. The words were literally jumping off the pages and landing on my heart.

One night, I was lying in bed and I realized that I needed to act on the words that I had read in the Bible. I wanted a full life in everything that the Word promised, and I wanted to go to heaven. I needed to ask Jesus into my heart.

Jesus said, "I am the way, the truth, and the life. No man comes to the father, but by me."

I believed those words and asked Jesus into my heart. I had never known such peace. And I've never been the same since.

From that point on, God became my true Father. For me, it wasn't about duty or religion. I've never belonged to any specific church. No, for me it was all about falling in love with God. The Lord became my biggest confidant. No matter how many mistakes I've made, how many times I've pulled away from God, He has never left me or forsaken me.

Over the years, I've been to a lot of different churches. I've listened to hundreds of sermons, and I'm still learning and growing. But when it comes to God, all too often people get caught up in rules and "looking good" or how they're perceived. If you say you're a Christian, then suddenly you can't drink wine or have fun. I think that's a big reason why so many people don't want anything to do with church or God, because they think they have to give up their fun. Or they think they are not good enough for God, so they decide to wait until they get "better" and then they'll think about God.

There's nothing you can do that makes you good enough.

Isaiah 64:6 talks about how all of our righteous acts are like filthy rags. In other words, we can't work our way into God's love. It's given to us. It's God's grace, not how we dress, whether we drink alcohol or cuss or have a tattoo or attend church services multiple times a week. Only God's grace can save us. Not ourselves and definitely no other man.

I think one of Satan's greatest tools is to convince people that being religious means having to follow all of these rules. Religion is man's attempt to get to God, while God's way to man is through relationship. If anyone tells you that you need anything other than the cross or Jesus, what they are saying is false, plain and simple.

I'm raising my children this way, too, and I can't tell you how many times people have thought that we aren't Christians because we don't always go to church and don't do the kids' Bible clubs. But I've always taught my kids that it's about your heart and how you treat other people, not about being seen in church. They know there are three things I cannot stand: lying, hypocrisy, and cruelty. There are two rules that we follow, found in the Gospels: to love God with all your heart and love your neighbor as yourself. Twice recently, one of my daughters had her faith questioned by others because of not being involved in church and for having a friend who is agnostic. That's not what the Bible teaches at all. Jesus preached love and forgiveness and kindness and hanging out with the unlikely ones.

∾

Back in Nashville after I accepted Christ into my heart, nothing instantly changed in my life. I actually struggled even more. But that's not what salvation is about. Jesus is not Santa Claus. The reason we obey God is because we love him, not because of what we are going to get from him. It's not about getting rid of sin or becoming perfect all of a sudden. Having a relationship with God means that you gain so much more than you can imagine. When you have God in your life, He works on your heart and changes the things that you enjoy. The things you once thought were fun might not be as exciting or interesting to you when you discover the richness of knowing God. Or maybe they still will be. That's between you and God. In other words, no person should ever come between you and God.

I won't tell you what you should believe or how you should live your life, but I do want to emphasize the importance of knowing God. Not a religion or church or certain pastor but God, through His Son, Jesus Christ.

I had accepted Jesus into my heart and found a relationship with

God, but I wasn't necessarily happy. My music career still wasn't taking off, but I felt different. I knew that I had God and that no matter what, I was going to be all right. Knowing this brought me immense joy and peace. And boy, did I need to believe that, because "hard times were coming!"

Chapter 8

NO PLACE THAT FAR

I t was a disaster. Country radio wasn't playing my music. *Three Chords and the Truth* didn't have one single hit reach the Top 40.

With that seven-album deal, everyone expected the first album to be a huge success. Instead, it was a disappointment. I was depressed, humiliated, frustrated, and, frankly, pissed. I refused to accept defeat. I immediately started writing for the next album. I decided to bring my music more center, to make it a little more commercial. It was cookie-cutter country that they wanted, so I was going to do everything in my power to be as cookie-cutter as I could without compromising my musical values.

I wrote a song called "No Place That Far" with Tom Shapiro and Tony Martin, two men who were at least twenty years older than me and had a lot of success writing country songs. The three of us hit it off, and since then, we've had four huge hits together. "No Place That

Far" was a safe song to take to radio as my next first single from my new album of the same title. It was released in 1998.

Joe Galante was not someone to accept failure, either. He came up with a plan to bring all the bigwigs at country radio together for a private concert with me in Cincinnati, Ohio. He flew everyone in, first-class, fed them a gourmet meal, filled them with alcohol, and made them sit in a small room and listen to me sing. We used to joke that Joe Galante, being from New York and also being Italian—you didn't mess with him. If you get my meaning.

I wasn't nervous for this performance—I was indignant. I already felt a ton of apathy toward these people, and that gave me courage, almost to the point of cockiness. By this time, Matt had moved back to Nashville and was playing bass for me and running the band, so I had the support from him that had always given me strength. Even though we aren't from New York and we aren't Italian, you don't mess with the Evanses, either.

Joe's plan worked. By the end of that show, they were all eating out of my hands and singing my praises. "No Place That Far" went to No. 1.

Again, I thought my career was taking off, but, lo and behold, radio betrayed me once again. They wouldn't play my next single—a cool, radio-friendly song that I wrote with Matraca Berg called "Fool, I'm a Woman." It was my second single on the album. People used to say in Nashville that a hit record can cure cancer. They also say that all it takes is three hits in a row. In other words, you need three hit singles to "make it and become a star."

It felt like I was constantly starting over, like in *Groundhog Day*, with these people in country radio. It was so hurtful to me, to my family, my band, and the people who'd believed in me. A bitterness started growing inside of me. I knew that the music was great, but the gatekeepers were not letting me in.

I called home to my mom, and we both cried.

"Why are they doing that? Why won't they play your music?" my mom asked.

Her heart was breaking for her little girl who she knew deserved to be on country radio.

Given the battle that we were facing getting my songs played, Brenner decided to join forces with another manager. He was supposed to be someone who had had success with other big-name acts, and Brenner felt like with me having my first No. 1 record, things were starting to explode, and she needed some help and guidance from someone who had already been a manager for a while. She felt that she could benefit from his experience and advice. He was a cocky guy right from the get-go. You could just see the smarm oozing out of him. He thought he was a really big deal. And he came into the picture after we had already done all the really hard groundwork and were having a No. 1 record, so he strutted around like he had done something to make that happen. He annoyed me from the beginning. But you're still learning at that phase in your career.

I found out that I was pregnant with my first child, and I was so excited. I had always dreamed of being a mom, and I felt great about it, because I had followed my plan and waited until I had my first No. 1 record to start a family. I knew enough about the entertainment industry to know that "suits" aren't always happy when their artists or actresses get pregnant. I was feeling very nervous about telling my record label and managers, but naively I told myself that they would be happy for me. Brenner was thrilled for me and was a mom herself. But I didn't get the same response from the new manager. I called him to tell him my incredible news, and there were about ten seconds of silence before he responded with one word: "F*** . . ."

I hung up the phone and cried and cried and cried, and this

wouldn't be the first time I cried about having what should have been complete personal joy ripped out from under me by the people who were only concerned about making money off me. I fired the new manager the next day.

∞

When you have a failed single on an album like I had with "Fool, I'm a Woman," it's risky to keep pushing that whole album because radio is so shortsighted and always looking for reasons NOT to play your music, so that sometimes forces the label to go ahead and start a new album. We walked away from *No Place That Far* and began plans for another new album.

It was late summer 1999, I was very pregnant with my first baby, my due date was August 21, and I was lying on the couch watching CMT (Country Music Television). It was that stage of pregnancy when I just felt huge and disgusting. Faith Hill's video for "Breathe" came on, and then Martina McBride's video for "I Love You." Oh my gosh, they both looked so cute and adorable, and, being the competitive freak that I am, I sat up and literally said out loud to the TV in a very Scarlett O'Hara voice, "As God is my witness, when this baby is born, I'm going to lose this weight, grow my hair long, and make the best album Nashville has ever heard, and I'll NEVER feel this way again!"

I was scheduled to perform at the CMA (Country Music Association) Awards in September, just a few weeks after the birth, so that was also HUGE motivation for me!

I had gained a lot of weight. I had no idea how long nine months really could turn out to be if you're telling yourself that it's okay to eat for two. Which it's really not. But I was so unbelievably sick with each pregnancy, like to the point of panic, that I ate all the wrong foods, and too much of them, to comfort my nauseated stomach. I had an event at the Wildhorse Saloon that was already contracted just days after Avery was born. I definitely was not ready to be seen in public by anyone, much less industry people, but I also had to start getting ready for the CMAs. Well, I left Avery just for those few hours and went to perform a few songs at this event, and when it was over Brenner said to me, "Hey, the label said they are concerned about your weight and really want you to lose the baby weight as soon as possible, okay?"

I was stunned. Shocked. Hurt. Furious. I have always been super-sensitive about my weight and body image. Brenner knew that, so for her to say that to me, knowing that Avery wasn't even two weeks old, was very poor judgment on her part. I just said okay as she dropped me at my front door. I remember sitting in the rocking chair with Avery at 3:00 a.m. nursing him and sobbing. I was so mad that what should have been the most precious and exciting time of my life had been so badly tainted. A manager's job is to protect and fight for their artists. She should have told the label to shut up and give me the time I needed and not to worry about it. And she definitely shouldn't have told me what they said. I called her the next morning and said, "Brenner, I love you, but if you EVER tell me anything like that again, you're fired!" She totally understood and apologized. I think she knew the moment she told me how hurt I was and regretted it instantly.

As an artist, you can really get into the frame of mind that you are working for your manager or your label or your agent. Instead, they make money off your talent and the opportunities they bring you. The relationship can also be viewed as a partnership, but they tend to become friends, and sometimes they forget that they are supposed to be representing you and your interests. The easiest thing for a manager to do is say yes to others and apologize to the artist later.

The hardest thing for a manager to do is to tell people no. They want to be liked in the industry so that they get a good reputation and gain more clients.

I've been lucky with managers, for the most part. Brenner was amazing and a true friend and truly cared about me. Now Craig Dunn loves me like family and I trust him completely. I still have that little voice in the back of my mind that says, "Don't let anyone down." But I was learning to stand up for myself.

∞

During my pregnancy, this kick-ass female trio called the Dixie Chicks had come onto the scene. They had a sound that I just died over! I thought, I want to work with whoever produced them and develop my own version of this sound! The Dixie Chicks were kind of blue-grassy, which was where I'd started. Brenner said to me, "You should write with Marcus Hummon. He wrote two or three hit songs for the Dixie Chicks, like 'Cowboy Take Me Away' and 'Ready to Run.' Maybe he can help you develop the new album."

When Avery was about six weeks old, I invited Paul Worley, the producer on that Dixie Chicks album, to my home for dinner. I cooked him the special ham and cheese quiche that Brenner had taught me to make—one of the many things she taught me to cook—and her special salad, which my whole family calls "the Brenner salad."

We talked about my new album and he agreed to produce it. I was thrilled.

Then I said, "There's one thing I want you to do for me."

"What's that?" Paul asked, leaning back in his chair.

"There's a drummer that I love. Everything that he does resonates with me." I can play drums, too, so I'm always listening to bass and drums. "I want this guy for the album."

"Who is it?"

"His name is Matt Chamberlain," I said. "He played on the Wall-flowers record *Bringing Down the Horse*, but I don't know anything else about him."

This was before Google, so it was kind of hard to find him. Paul said, "Okay. I'll put Paige on it."

Paige was Paul's assistant. Together they found Matt Chamberlain living in Seattle. Turned out that Matt had played on a lot of amazing rock projects—Pearl Jam, Soundgarden, and the Edie Brickell & New Bohemians album *Shooting Rubberbands at the Stars*, which included "What I Am," a song I loved that had a really cool drum part.

"We found Matt Chamberlain, and he said he'd love to play on the album," Paul told me.

I said, "Okay. I'll start writing and you start looking for songs. Then we'll be in touch."

Soon after that, Marcus Hummon and Darrell Scott came out to the house. Since we'd only just met, Marcus said, "Sara, tell me about yourself."

I began with, "Well, I grew up on a farm in Missouri . . . "

Then we started writing. That's how, in 2000, "Born to Fly" came to be.

∞

This is one of those times I'm most proud of in my career. Mine was the first country album Matt Chamberlain ever played on. In fact, he never had even been to Nashville. His style of drumming is so unlike anyone else's, and he really played a huge role in helping me hone in on a specific sound for the *Born to Fly* album, and every album since then. After people heard *Born to Fly*, everyone started asking Matt to play the drums on their albums. Artists like Faith Hill, Keith Urban,

Martina McBride, and many others. But I love to brag about the fact that I brought him to Nashville first.

Born to Fly took us to the next level. Finally, country radio gave me the support I deserved. I had four hit singles off the album and sold five million copies. I was officially a star.

Everything in my life was amazing. I had the first true love of my life—my baby boy. I'd named him Avery Jack, after my dad. Becoming a mom was the absolute best thing that had ever happened to me personally. Also, I was skinny, my hair was long, I was finding my style, I was touring and doing every media opportunity, and I was making money, FINALLY. I still look at that time as one of the best times in my life, hands down.

Born to Fly was nominated for five CMA Awards that year: album of the year, song of the year, single of the year, video of the year, and

Born to Fly goes platinum! With Joe Galante
and Butch Waugh from RCA Records.

female vocalist of the year. I could also win another CMA award as a producer if *Born to Fly* won album of the year.

As luck would have it, the movie *O Brother, Where Art Thou?* was released that year, and its album swept the awards, which I thought was really unfair, because it wasn't in the genre. It was a movie soundtrack. But I did take home video of the year. The video was a take on *The Wizard of Oz*, and I posed as a sexy Dorothy dreaming of somewhere over the rainbow, which for me was Nashville, and country music stardom. Peter Zavadil directed it. My attitude has always been stick with what works, and since then, Peter has directed almost every one of my music videos.

I'll never forget the night of the CMAs. I felt like the darling of the event, with everyone talking about me because I had so many nominations. *Born to Fly* truly is an amazing album, and I am so proud of it. The media rushed over to interview me on the red carpet, and I realized that I'd really become a star—and not just a star, but an artist who was truly respected in the industry.

∞

For the next five years, I was living the dream—well, in every aspect except the one I couldn't talk about and still can't completely.

My name was at the top of the charts in country music, and I was on huge tours with artists like George Strait, Alan Jackson, and Reba McEntire. I also headlined my own tours, with up-and-comers like Josh Turner and Luke Bryan opening for me. For the first time in my life, my career was on fire!

I added two more children to my family with the births of my baby girls Olivia Margaret and Audrey Elizabeth, who were born just twenty months apart. Those years between 1999 and 2006 were a blur of making hit records and raising babies on the road. I've always taken my kids everywhere with me. They all learned to walk and talk and were potty-trained on a tour bus. They've been to every state except Alaska, and they've been to multiple countries. They are extremely mature for their ages because of being raised on the road.

I was so happy, and making and performing great music. *Born to Fly* was certified two-time platinum in the United States, and then *Restless* and *Real Fine Place*, my next two albums, were both certified platinum. Singles like "Perfect," "Suds in the Bucket," "A Real Fine Place to Start," and "Cheatin'" were all hits.

I had reached stardom. But one thing about stardom is that once you've reached it, you have to keep it going or it disappears fast. There are a lot of demands, and back then, I never said *no* to anything.

I was literally crushing life.

I had finally achieved the fairy tale I'd dreamed of.

Then another "*wah wah wah.*"

Chapter 9

MY BIGGEST FEAR

To the outside world, my life seemed absolutely perfect. But there was one secret that I kept from everyone, even my closest friends and family. I was miserable in my marriage.

I tried denying it to myself, and I tried to work on it. After the pain of being a child of divorce, I'd made a commitment to never divorce. And, of course, people who follow Jesus should not get divorced. I went to marriage counseling several different times off and on for three years, but it just wasn't working. My marriage was disintegrating before my eyes like a sandcastle when the tide comes in. Long story short, we were not right for each other, and I knew that if I didn't get out, it would be really bad for me.

This all became abundantly clear when, in December 2005, I had a meltdown.

∞

Women are prone to overdoing it, giving too much, trying to do it all. We take on more than we should and put the needs of everyone else before our own. I was balancing motherhood, a failing marriage, three young kids on the road with me, and an extremely demanding career. I was determined not to let country radio have any excuse not to play me. I didn't see the signs that I was headed for a crash.

I had just made *Real Fine Place* and launched it, and I dove into something like 298 appearances in one year in my attempt to do everything I could to keep the success going. My goal has always been to make enough money to leave a great inheritance and legacy for my children. I said yes to everything and forgot there was a "too far." Or maybe I just didn't want to admit I was going there.

I was raising my three young kids with a nanny in tow while I performed and promoted my album. Audrey was a baby and Olivia a toddler, and Avery was in kindergarten. Parenting kids this age is challenging enough at home, but I felt like a single mom out on the road and living in a bus—a very nice bus, and with great people around us, but still the situation was draining. My nanny helped, and I was lucky to have her, but she was not a parent. She was a person being paid to take care of my kids, and that's a big difference. My band was there, too, including my brother Matt, who was like a surrogate father out on the road. He'd married Kaelin, or KK as Avery would start calling her and her name to this day, who was like another sister to me. She'd later become my stylist and is still with me at every show and event. But even with their help, the demand was just too great for any human being to fulfill.

Album launches are grueling because you have to do a lot of things that are out of the normal routine of touring. In order to sell a ton of records the first week and subsequently debut at the top of the album charts, you try to get as much press as possible during that first week. This was where the details and each conversation with the press really mattered. It was a huge push, and I had to be *on* all of the time. This meant being able to sing and smile and be ready for any surprise question from an interviewer.

At the same time I was doing all of that, I was also on a major tour, opening up for Brad Paisley. So there were days that I would do press all day and then do my show that night, all the while trying to squeeze in moments with my babies. I mean, they were there, but I wasn't really. I was exhausted and occupied and stressed! I had a day off from the tour in Pennsylvania, and I needed to go into New York for some publicity. The kids were settled in fine, but leaving my babies on a day off felt like torture. The plan was to stay overnight in New York and then return to them in Pennsylvania the next day. I wanted to cry when I left them, but I soldiered on.

I headed into the city to a packed day of media appearances. I did the showcase that night and finally collapsed in the hotel. I wanted to call the kids, but they would already be asleep. Sometimes calling them was added torture, because it just made me miss them that much more, and I couldn't bear to hear them say, "I miss you, Mommy. When will you be back?" I wanted to be there, to experience their day, to put them to bed and hold their soft little hands. I craved having my babies in my arms or asleep on my shoulder.

My sister Lesley had flown to New York City with me to do some acoustic performances, and we shared a hotel room that night, and a bed. At my request. I could feel myself coming apart, and my band and crew and family could, too. I didn't want to be alone that night, and anyone who has a sister knows that getting in the bed with her to be cozy and talk is the best remedy for stress. I told Lesley that night that I was having a lot of anxiety and that I felt like I couldn't get a grasp on who I was. It's a feeling that I have struggled with my whole life anytime I am stressed. I think it's PTSD from getting hit by a car. I have this feeling of "who am I?" It tends to creep up on me after I've had to do a lot of interviews and be on and play the part of "Sara Evans." I don't even like writing about it because I am so afraid of having this feeling.

The next morning, Lesley had an early flight back home to Missouri, so she left before I woke up. I had a car service waiting to drive me to Pennsylvania to meet my bus and the kids. I was so excited to finally be done with the press stuff and just get back to the buses with everyone.

I said hello to the driver as I slipped into the car. I noticed him glance at me as we took off. I knew there wasn't anything wrong with the guy. I told myself this again and again. Surely car services like this did background checks on their drivers. But what if? What if he wasn't a good guy? My anxious mind started creating story after awful story in my head. As we drove out of the city, my terrifying thoughts were building. Did he recognize me? Did anyone know where I was right now? If I disappeared, how long until they'd start looking?

I wanted to get to my kids so badly. They were just babies. What if this guy drove me off into the woods and killed me? What if he had a gun or a knife under his seat? What would happen to my babies then? My mind was going crazy with anxiety. The truth was, I was falling apart and didn't fully realize it.

The farther we drove, the more terrified I felt. I flipped down the fold-down mirror from the car celing and looked at the eyes staring back at me. My eyes. I knew they were supposed to be my eyes, but I did not truly recognize them or my face or anything about myself. I stared, and that person stared back. It had to be me in the mirror, but who was "me"? I could see my hands moving, but I didn't recognize them. I wanted to cry. My heart was racing, and I couldn't catch my breath.

I rolled the window down and stuck my head out, trying to draw in deep breaths. The driver said, "Are you okay? Do you need me to pull over?"

"No! I'm just having a little anxiety. I'll be fine," I said.

I had about another hour in the car to get through, and I'm sure the driver was nervous about whether I'd make it to our destination without him having to make a turn into the nearest ER. Most of the drive I was gasping for air or had my head sticking out the window, my cheek resting on the door.

Somehow, I made it to Pennsylvania. I saw the bus and got out of the car, but my body felt drained and strangely not my own. The kids were so excited to see me, and somehow, I went through the motions. They were too young to notice. My sweet nanny, Katie, instantly saw that something was not right.

I told her I'd just had a panic attack and still felt like I was panicking. The bus felt too confining, so we decided to go straight to a Christian bookstore in the mall, because I wanted to get a Bible. I didn't know exactly what was happening to me, but I knew that whatever it was, I needed to reach out to my heavenly Father for help and healing. So my tour manager arranged for all of us to go to the mall.

I also hoped the mall might ground me in normalcy and give the kids an outlet to move their little legs and pick out some toys, maybe get ice cream—anything to take my mind off the inexplicable fear and dread that I was feeling. I tried to act like everything was fine, but I had this sense that I wasn't really there, as if I were a wisp of air and nothing more. I felt completely disassociated from myself.

That evening before I went into hair and makeup, I called my mom, and as soon as I heard her voice, I started crying. It's amazing how much comfort a mother can give. I said, "Mommy, I need you. I am so exhausted and overworked and stressed, and I've been having such horrible anxiety, and I have that feeling again that I don't know who I am." I had told her about these feelings throughout my life. She was always great at talking me off the ledge. "Tell me about being born," I said.

She immediately knew what I needed to hear. "You were born on February fifth, nineteen seventy-one. I promise," she said. "You are real and you know who you are. You are just exhausted and stressed, and you are about to get a good long break, right?" I said, "Yes, we have the show tonight and then two more shows and then we are off until the new year." Mom also suggested that I get Brenner to find a doctor who could prescribe something for my anxiety. We were able to find someone, and that helped me get through the performances. But I still had to keep turning and looking back at Matt during those last three shows to remind myself that I was real, that he was real, and that this awful feeling was all in my head.

Finally, we headed back home to Nashville. I was hoping that just being home and having some much-needed rest would make it all better, but it didn't. I went to see a doctor and he prescribed me an anti-depressant (which I never took, because I knew I wasn't depressed; I was exhausted). He also prescribed an anti-anxiety medication that is non–habit forming and was really perfect for me. It really helped calm the anxiety and panic, but I knew this was a much deeper issue. For about ten days straight I was afraid to leave my house. Actually, I was afraid to walk from one room to another. All I did was sit in front of the fireplace with the girls playing around me and read my Bible. I was totally consumed with fear. And for no reason. I remember just dreading the hour when Avery was going to be getting off the school bus from kindergarten, because I knew I would have to pretend that everything was fine and it most certainly was not. The girls were both babies, so they had no idea. But I was so afraid that Avery would catch on and then start being afraid himself.

I knew that something in my subconscious was causing this fear and that I needed to figure out what it was. So I called my pastor, Dave, and explained what was going on and told him that I needed him to come to my house and pray over me. He came over every day for several days in a row, and we prayed and read Scripture and talked. He knew me well because he had done some marriage counseling for us as well. He encouraged me just to stay at home for the time being and get rest and let God do the rest.

My sister Ashley had struggled with postpartum depression after the birth of her second child, and she completely understood what I was going through. Anxiety is something that is so real and yet so baffling; you know in your reasonable mind that there is nothing to be afraid of, but you are afraid. You're terrified of nothing. I had a feeling, though. I knew what it was.

Musicians regularly end up in the hospital, and it becomes a big media flurry. People balk at the diagnosis of "exhaustion," but I can attest to the truth of it. Thankfully, mine never made the news, although little did I know I would have plenty of that ahead.

∞

I knew I had to address what was happening in my life. I couldn't push myself that hard anymore, especially not while being a mom and wanting to create a wonderful life with my children. I knew that my marriage was beyond repair. But how in the world could I even contemplate divorce when my parents' divorce had hurt me so badly? I didn't want my children to come from a broken home. I wanted them to have an idyllic life within the perfect family. This was so important to me—essential to the vision I had for my life. But sometimes things are simply out of our control.

I know now that what I was experiencing is called depersonalization. There were signs I could have noticed if I'd known what to look for. There were signs my family and friends could have noticed. But none of us really knew how to spot them, and I was very good at pretending I was fine.

Looking back, I know that my breakdown was also God telling me to stop and examine different aspects of my life. I know that what happened to me in December 2005 was a blessing in disguise. I learned a lesson through that season, but I have to admit, I didn't learn it well enough. In 2014, I went through a similar experience. This time I thought I could push beyond my limits because I was in a great marriage and my kids had a stable home. This deceived me into thinking I could do everything that was expected of me to be successful in my career. I couldn't.

Today, I've learned to be smart about myself. I know I can convince everyone around me that I'm okay. I now can pull myself together and put on my game face when underneath, all is not well. But the only person who is responsible for my health is me. Not my husband, not my friends, not my mother or my manager or even my doctor. I have to be responsible about my own health and well-being. I need to pay attention to the signs of burnout. I need to listen to God about what I should and shouldn't do, and trust Him when doors close or open. I know God took care of me and my kids during those dark times, and He'll take care of me always. But understanding my limits is an important part of being my best and being able to perform at my highest ability.

Today, I'm much more into self-care, and it's something I encourage you to look at in your own life, too. A woman is such an anchor inside the home, setting the emotional climate, whether for good or for bad. If you think you can be stretched beyond your limit, or that continually sacrificing yourself will bring good to your family, you're wrong. If you want your home to be nurturing, warm, loving, exciting, and stable, then you have to care for yourself so you can care for everyone else.

∞

In 2006, I was back on my feet, still working with marriage counselors to try to keep my marriage going, when I received an invitation to be on *Dancing with the Stars*.

I was so excited! I had already become a fan of the show and couldn't believe that I was going to be one of the stars competing. One of the first things that happens is that they schedule a day for their camera crews to come film you while you meet your dance partner so they can get your true reactions. I had decided that the best thing for our marriage during this time would be for us to stay at our little farmhouse in Oregon, so I asked if we could rehearse for the debut show out there. They found us a dance studio in Salem, Oregon, and that is where I met Tony Dovolani for the first time.

We immediately became best friends. He was so funny and just about eighteen months younger than me, and we looked good dancing together. Both dark, with dark hair. They matched us perfectly. We had a lot of work to do, so I would meet him at the studio every morning around 9:00 a.m. and we would dance until I started getting antsy to get home to my babies, which wasn't a very long time. I've always been such a hands-on mom, and I HATED being away from my kids for more than a few hours at a time. At this time Avery was seven, Olivia was three, and Audrey was two. I was also the only mom competing that season. So I couldn't rehearse as long each day as some of the others. But I busted my butt when we did rehearse.

Tony was born in Kosovo to Albanian parents, and he is Muslim. I was fascinated when he told me all about his childhood and also how dancing was so popular and considered to be very manly. He has a beautiful wife—I remember meeting her for the first time and just being in awe of her beauty and thinking what a cute couple they were.

After the few weeks spent in Oregon rehearsing, we all moved to Beverly Hills, into the house that *DWTS* had rented for us. It was gorgeous, and I was on cloud nine. I still had shows booked that I couldn't cancel, so the schedule was rigorous. The kids and I would either get on the bus or fly to do the shows, and then come back to LA. There were a lot of requirements from *DWTS*, like interviews for the packages they would put together for each episode, a dress rehearsal/camera-blocking day, and then the actual show day, with a string of interviews after each show.

It was absolutely exhausting and totally invigorating at the same time. I loved every minute of it. At first the judges were not nice to me at all, and I think this inspired my fans to pick up the phone and vote for me. After the very first dance, one of the judges told me I moved like Barbara Bush. The second week they were still very critical—they kept telling me I was too conservative and needed to loosen up. And then it was time for the dance that really changed the way the judges saw me, the jive! If memory serves me, the show also chooses the song that you get to dance to each week, and for our jive they chose Nancy Sinatra's "These Boots Are Made for Walkin'." We thought, "This is perfect! We will dress up in cowboy and cowgirl clothes and put that spin on it." So Tony had the brilliant idea of having the camera start on his boot, with my nail-polished hands slowly moving up the boot until it reached his hairy leg, and then the camera would show us with a "we're just kidding! That was Tony's leg, not Sara's!" kind of look on our faces, and then the song would start and off we would go.

Tony choreographed the perfect dance for me. I grew up doing country dances like the two-step and the triple, and of course I spent hours watching people do these dances, so this was in my wheelhouse. My outfit was a white button-down bedazzled shirt with a blue bedazzled bra, and a blue bedazzled skirt, with brown bedazzled boots and a brown bedazzled cowboy hat. I wore my hair super-long with a bunch of added extensions, and board-straight. I looked amazing and the outfit was sexy. Very sexy. We killed it! I mean, the crowd was absolutely on their feet before the last note was struck! You could just tell by the feeling in the room that I had changed the judges' and the fans' minds. I was now legit in this competition. The judges sang my praises and we got all 10s that night. We were so happy.

After that, I kept making it week after week to the next round. It was really getting intense. But it was getting intense at home, too. It was becoming increasingly clear that my efforts to repair the marriage could not hold off the inevitable. There were times that I would sit in the chair in the makeup trailer and they would almost have my makeup completely done, and someone would say, "Are you okay?" and I would burst into tears and they would have to fix my running mascara and tear-streaked heavy foundation. With the competition and the work and my babies, I had made it easier to avoid admitting what was really going on. Then one night it all blew up between my husband and me, and I knew that I would not be able to finish *DWTS*. I had to quit working altogether, focus on my children, and really figure out what I was going to do. I had some tough decisions to make. So I called Brenner and said, you need to get me out of the show. I can't do this anymore, because my kids need me right now, every second

After dancing the jive with Tony Dovolani

of every day. The show couldn't have been more understanding—all they asked was that I do a short interview with host Tom Bergeron to explain my departure.

Divorce is one of the hardest things a person can go through. In marriage, life is so intertwined with another human being, especially if you have children together. In divorce, you begin the process of untangling the thread that was holding you together. I had no idea how hard it was actually going to be, and being famous while going through it was excruciating. I had so much fear and anxiety about the future and what the divorce would do to my kids. Those next several weeks were a blur. And I still had touring dates that I had to fulfill.

I called my sisters, Lesley and Ashley, and asked them if they could come out on tour with me and start singing harmony, and just be there with me. I don't know what I would have done without my family during that time. There were a few times when I had to be on stage at 9:00 p.m. and I couldn't get out of my bunk to even get ready. I remember calling Brenner and begging her to cancel a show because I was too sad and scared to go on stage. But somehow I forced myself to get up and do my job. Every day got a little easier, and every day I got a little bit stronger.

Chapter 10

THE BARKER BUNCH

In the autumn of 2007, I'd settled into a good routine with my three kids as a single mom. It had been almost a year since I'd filed for divorce, but it was taking forever to finalize.

I was on the bus out on tour when a marriage counselor I had met with several times named Joe Beam called me one night. My three kids were sleeping in their bunks, and I was up front with my sisters watching a chick flick and having a glass of wine after a sold-out show in Chicago.

Joe said something like, "Hi, Sara, just calling to check in on you to see how you are doing, and to tell you that I counseled a man who I think would be perfect for you."

I choked on my red wine.

I said, "What? I'm sorry Joe, I think you have the wrong number. I'm never getting married again."

He laughed and said, "I understand, but something about this guy is very special, so once your divorce is final, call me. I want to meet with you and talk to you about this guy. He's gone through a similar situation as you. He's a celebrity, he has four children, he's a great father, a strong believer, and my wife says he's very handsome." Then he added, "I've never met two people more alike, and I thought at the very least you could be support systems for each other and good friends."

I said, "Thanks, but no thanks. I appreciate you thinking of me, but like I said, I'm never getting married again."

When I got home from that tour, I decided to go have coffee with Joe because, as they say, *curiosity killed the cat*. I simply couldn't resist finding out who this mysterious "great guy" was that Joe had in mind for me. We met at Starbucks in downtown Franklin, Tennessee. When he walked in, I noticed that Joe had a manila envelope tucked under his arm. We exchanged pleasantries, and he opened the envelope as though he were a CIA agent about to show me a file on my new hit job.

He said, "This is Jay Barker. He's from Birmingham, Alabama. He was the quarterback at the University of Alabama and won the national championship title for them in 1992 as a sophomore. He went on to play with the NFL for several years, and now he does a sports talk show in Birmingham."

Joe had several articles about Jay. Joe's wife was right, this guy was very handsome—actually gorgeous.

Joe said, "Last year, I went to Alabama and counseled with Jay as he was going through his divorce. I'm telling you, Sara, he's the male version of you, and you are the female version of him. I've never done anything like this before." He meant he'd never matched two people whose marriages he had attempted to save.

I was still very skeptical and just couldn't imagine putting forth the energy it would take to date someone.

After we finished catching up, Joe prayed over me. I went back home with that manila envelope in my purse.

On the day that my divorce was final, I was in the kitchen doing dishes after putting the kids to bed. And it was like the Holy Spirit grabbed me by my arm and pulled me to my home office.

I opened that manila envelope and drafted an email to Jay Barker. *Hey Jay, it's Sara Evans. Our mutual friend Joe Beam gave me your contact info. I just wanted to say that I'm so sorry for everything you've been through. My divorce was final today. If you ever want to talk, I'm here.*

I hesitated and then hit send.

Within five minutes, I heard my computer ding. It was Jay.

Hey Sara, it's Jay Barker. Nice to meet you. Thank you so much for your email. It has been a really hard last couple of years. Wow, my divorce was final today as well. I would love to talk. Is it okay if I call you tomorrow?

We talked every day after that for three weeks. Our talks lasted hours and hours. We were soaking up every bit of information we could get from each other.

It wasn't long before I could tell that I was falling in love with this man over the phone. Finally, he said, "Can I come up to Nashville and take you on a proper date?"

Our first date was October 3, 2007, just three days before my youngest, Audrey, turned three.

Growing up, I played basketball, softball, and ran track. I was a really good athlete. I had a feeling that I'd impress Jay if we did something athletic.

I said, "Why don't we meet at the park near my house and throw a softball?"

Jay seemed to like that idea. Or maybe he thought it was weird, but he agreed.

∞

I wore faded bell-bottom jeans, a hippie-type shirt that I got at Urban Outfitters, and flip-flops. We met at Fieldstone Park in Franklin. When Jay pulled up, he got out of his truck looking like a 6'3", 220-pound model. He wore a baseball cap, t-shirt, True Religion jeans with holes in the knees, and motorcycle boots. His pictures did not do him justice. He was stunning, with royal blue eyes. I was a goner.

I said, "Did you bring your glove?"

"Sure did." He grabbed his mitt from his truck.

We looked at the other's mitts and realized we had the same Cooper glove. We'd even written our names in the identical spots on the palm of the glove. His said *Barker* and mine said *Evans*. I remembered how Joe Beam had said that Jay was the male version of me, and I was the female version of Jay.

At first, Jay would only lob balls to me. I guess he thought I was a girlie girl. Finally, I said, "What are you doing? Throw the ball!"

"Are you sure?" he asked.

"Yes, I'm sure."

So Jay threw a really hard ball that hit the dirt right in front of me, and I scooped it up and fired it back at him. He took his glove off and feigned pain. And I could tell that he was a goner, too.

It was unseasonably hot for October, so we threw for a little while longer and decided to get dinner. We went to a little restaurant called Puckett's in Franklin, sat outside, and ordered cheeseburgers and fries. I couldn't stop looking at his beautiful face. There was a speaker right over our heads with loud, annoying music, and I had a hard time hearing him with the music and with his deep southern drawl. I kept leaning in closer to hear him, and later, Jay told me that he couldn't tell if I was trying to kiss him or not, but that he thought it would be too forward to kiss me. And he didn't kiss me at all that first night, because he's a gentleman.

Neither of us could deny that Joe Beam was right. We were made for each other. We had a very fast courtship. I think when you are dating in your thirties, you just know who you are and who you want to be with. It's much easier than it is when you're in your twenties. By January, we were secretly planning our wedding.

In March there's a week called CRS (Country Radio Seminar) when all the artists come together and spend days doing interviews and liners for radio. Every year, RCA hosts all the radio programmers and VIPs on a showboat called the *General Jackson*, where they are entertained by RCA's artists and newly signed acts. We call it "the boat show," and it's really exhausting. The boat takes off from downtown Nashville and goes all the way out to Opryland and then back. Joe Galante was brilliant in starting this, because once the radio bigwigs agree to come to the boat show, they are trapped and cannot get away until the boat docks. I'm sure it's a really fun night for them. They get a great meal, and an open bar, and a star-filled show.

It's something I dreaded every year because I would be so nervous around all the radio guys. You have to be really careful that you do and say all the right things, and if you're selected to perform that year, you have to be really impressive. You can't do anything to turn off any radio programmer and risk that they won't play your single. One day we were on one of the whirlwind radio tours and I was full of anxiety, away from my kids, and on an elevator with my label rep and a radio guy. As I've said, I am SO claustrophobic and I am terrified of elevators. Just the thought of getting stuck in one makes my heart start racing. I said to them, "I'm just going to look at my phone for a minute, not trying to be rude, but I need a distraction to keep me from being terrified right now." Well, I guess the radio guy didn't hear me say that, and he thought I was being rude by looking at my phone, so he wouldn't play my single. His decision kept that song from reaching the Top 5.

It was the night of the annual RCA boat show, and I had just gotten off the boat and was headed back to my bus when Jay texted me that he was almost to Nashville from Birmingham. I said, "What? Why? What are you doing here?" He said that he wanted to see me. I told him to come to my bus and pick me up and take me home. On the way home, he pulled into the park where we'd had our first date. I said, "What are you doing!"

He said, "Just get out and come with me." It was around 11:30 p.m., and the gate had been locked to close off the park for the night. We climbed over it, and he got down on one knee and said something like, "Sara, you are the best person I have ever known. You have become my best friend, and I love you with all of my heart. I want to spend the rest of my life with you. Will you marry me?" And he presented me with the most beautiful ring I've ever seen. And I, of course, said YES.

On June 14, 2008, we officially became Mr. and Mrs. Jay Barker. Our wedding took place on a beautiful farm outside Franklin, beside a lake. We didn't want the press to get wind of where the wedding was, so everyone met at a designated location and we bused them to the farm.

∞

Jay has four kids—three boys and a girl. Together, we have seven children—three girls and four boys. The three girls wore white sundresses with yellow flowers and black sashes. Our boys wore black polo shirts with white khaki pants. Everyone wore flip-flops.

KK and I had started dress shopping back in the winter, and I'd chosen a beautiful ivory taffeta gown by Vera Wang. Jay wore a Dolce & Gabbana suit that was tailor-made to fit his amazing athletic physique.

Jay's kids escorted him toward the altar and stood waiting for me, and then my kids escorted me and we all met at the altar.

We'd wheeled a baby grand out to the grass, and my sweet friend Marcus Hummon sang "Bless the Broken Road," a Rascal Flatts hit that he'd cowritten. The lyrics meant a lot to Jay and me. Then my sisters, Lesley and Ashley, harmonized on a song called "Feels Like Home" written by Randy Newman. There wasn't a dry eye at the entire wedding.

We recited vows we both wrote to each other. Things like:

> *I promise to love your children as my own*
> *I promise to help you raise your children*
> *I promise to be faithful to you*
> *I promise to laugh with you*
> *I promise to have fun with you . . .*

I also promised Jay that I would treat him like a king, and he promised me that he would treat me like a queen. After we kissed, we all walked back up the aisle as a family of nine.

For the reception, we had southern fried chicken, mashed potatoes and gravy, country-style pole beans, biscuits, and macaroni and cheese. We sent everyone home with a peach pie. We danced till two in the morning. I only remember dancing with Jay the whole time.

There was a cabin on the property that my wedding planner turned into a wedding suite for us. There was a king-size mattress on the floor with a brand-new heavy white comforter, and the cabin was stocked with wine and lit by a dozen candles. All the things I requested. No television, no phones, just the two of us.

Jay and I spent the first week after the wedding at home with the kids in Franklin. It reminded me of the first episode of *The Brady Bunch*, where the newlywed parents, Mike and Carol, leave for their honeymoon, but, once there, Carol confesses that she is worried about leaving the kids so soon after the wedding—especially after Fluffy the cat had gotten loose at the reception and Tiger the dog chased her, knocking over the wedding cake. So, just like Mike and Carol Brady, we didn't want to leave our seven children after such an emotional thing had happened—their parents had gotten married. I'm sure it also had something to do with my memories of my parents remarrying. I didn't want to be oblivious to the feelings of my kids and new stepchildren.

After a week of playing sports and games together, Jay's kids went

The Barker Bunch

back to their mom, and my kids stayed with Matt and KK. Then we went to Fisher Island off the coast of Miami for our honeymoon.

While we were on our honeymoon, my sister Ashley and KK and my assistant moved us into our new home, in Mountain Brook, Alabama, near Birmingham. When we came home, we were ready to start our new life together.

Ten years later, I feel like we're still on our honeymoon.

Chapter 11

SWEET HOME ALABAMA

Moving from Nashville to the Birmingham area seemed so right for me personally but so wrong professionally. I did it for Jay and his children. He was willing to move to Nashville, but he didn't come from a divorced family, so he didn't understand what moving to another state could do to his relationship with his kids. He thought, "I can make that work," but I knew that if I really loved him I had to think about his kids and what I went through. I remembered when my dad moved to Dallas. I would've been such a hypocrite if I'd encouraged Jay to move to Nashville and leave his kids in Birmingham.

I knew that the distance would eventually take a toll and that slowly we'd start missing things in their lives. We would've settled into our work and our life together, and it would be easy to say, "You know, I don't think we're going to be able to make it to this game or that event or get them this weekend. There's just so much going on." It would become more and more of a habit, even if we'd started out with good intentions. I knew Jay's kids eventually would've hated me, and they would have hated my kids if we'd taken their dad away from them.

So I made that decision because I chose to marry a man with children who was from another state, and I wanted us to be a family. My kids were still really little, under age eight. The girls hadn't started school yet, and Avery was almost done with second grade when I decided to move.

Being such a perfectionist, my dream was to perfect the blended family. I started trying so hard to make every weekend and Wednesday night and every other week in the summer, and every other holiday, just fun, fun, fun. All the time. I desperately wanted our seven kids to be happy, and most of all to feel LOVED. That's all I've ever wanted. The role of a stepparent is not to act like the parent. The press and the media will write things about me being a mom to seven. I'm not a mom to seven. I'm a mom to three, and a stepmom to four. And that's something that I really want to stress. I have never said that I'm raising Jay's kids. I have never tried to suggest that all seven kids live with us full-time. I think the media likes to say that because it makes for a more interesting story. The Barker Bunch story. But I'm their stepmom, not their mom. And I like to think of myself as an aunt or older sister, or a mentor to them. I'm there for them if they ever need anything, but I'm not their mom, and I don't try to be.

Professionally, moving to Alabama was a much bigger sacrifice than I realized it would be. It's more expensive for me to live in Alabama, because anytime I need to go to Music Row, I have to drive up or use my bus. The Birmingham airport has practically no direct flights anywhere, so for all of our travel, we have to go through

Atlanta, and it can be challenging getting the limited flights in and out. It's a lot more travel cost because the band and crew buses all leave from Nashville, and Chris, my driver of fourteen years, has to come to Birmingham a day early to get his sleep and then be able to get us at midnight to leave for the tour run. But I did it for love, and I'm really glad I did. Mountain Brook has been an amazing little idyllic place to raise my kids.

∾

It's a beautiful southern town with winding roads, creeks, and thick forested hillsides woven around some of the oldest homes and mansions in the country. It's made up of three villages—Crestline Village, Mountain Brook Village, and English Village. We found a house in Crestline Village right across the field from the elementary school. That field was like our front yard. We did everything on it. We played softball, baseball, football, Ultimate Frisbee, tag, volleyball without a net—you name it, we played it. My favorite thing to do is have Jay hit pop flies that are out-of-this-world high, catch them, and then sling them back to him. It's an amazing workout, and I used to love to show off when other people were on the field. At first they would stare, because we were new celebrities who had just moved to their town, but then they would stare because they couldn't believe what they were watching. Have I told you I'm a great athlete?

We could walk everywhere around town, to shops or the restaurants. It felt like a fairy tale when we moved here. Our life was wonderful. Ten years later, Mountain Brook, Alabama, is where my children have grown up. This is their childhood hometown, and it feels like home for me, too, at least for now. Sometimes I dream of buying a farm or a big horse ranch, and Jay and I have talked about moving back to Nashville once our kids are all grown. But being in Mountain

Brook has brought me so much joy, and a lot of other things as well, including great friends.

Since moving here I've made some of the best friends I've ever had. I can't imagine my life without my four best friends. I have lots of awesome friends, but these four are the ones I am closest to and have spent the most time with.

I now understand how important friendships are. I really think women put too much pressure on their marriages and talk to their husbands about a lot of things we shouldn't—like our weight, friend drama, PMS problems, and just other silly stuff that they don't care about. Women can talk literally all day about a million things, and men don't work like that. Men are not emotional like women, so we shouldn't expect them to be. I NEVER tell Jay when I think I'm fat. I don't want to put that in his head! I only want him to see me at my best, and I want him to think that I am confident, because that is sexy.

Some of the sexiest things to me in a man are confidence, authenticity, honesty, kindness, and masculinity. Don't freak out. I'm not talking about what everyone has been saying recently—"toxic masculinity." To me, being masculine means being a great guy, a kind

Jay and me

and loving husband, and a hard worker, and being honest, taking care of your family, being a good father, and being brave. Knowing what the people in your circle need, and caring about those needs. I don't want Jay coming home and unloading his stress on me. That's what his buddies are for. They can go have a beer and talk about things that are stressing them out or worrying them. I want my man to be the man, and I want to be the woman. Maybe that's not for everyone, but that's how we function.

It kind of sounds like I don't want a "real" relationship. I do, just not too real. I think in order to keep the attraction alive you have to draw lines and have boundaries. Like using the bathroom in front of each other, OMG GROSS! People, do not do that. To me that would kill all chances of romance. I'm lucky because my husband is hot. He has great genes, and he looks great all the time. But no matter how attracted you are to someone physically, they can still turn you off if they aren't careful. Jay knows that I don't like to be asked a lot of questions, and I have always made that clear. But his family are question askers! "Where are the paper towels?" "In the kitchen closet, third shelf." "This closet?" "Yes." "Right here?" "YES." "Did you say third shelf?" "I'LL JUST GET THEM MYSELF!!!!!!!!!!!!!!!" So if he ever starts going down that road, I'll get this stressed look on my face, even when I don't know it, and he will say, "Oh yeah, too many questions." And we laugh about it. Sometimes it makes me feel like a bitch, but I just can't handle a lot of questions. I think it's rude. On their part, not mine.

I don't like to be shown things, either. You know how some people just LIVE to show you things? Something they saw on Facebook or Insta or YouTube? It's fine once in a while, especially if it's something incredible, but when you monopolize a family get-together or interrupt a conversation to show me something, it takes all of my good

upbringing and manners to grit my teeth, smile, and say, "Sure I'd love to see it."

So it's knowing the little things that can really help a marriage. If your spouse tells you these things, REALLY try to listen and not be annoying. That's a turnoff. Also, I hate laziness. I detest it, ESPECIALLY in a man. If you want to lose all of my respect as a man, be lazy or irresponsible. Or lie. Game over.

Back to my girlfriends. One of the many reasons I bonded so quickly with these four women is that we all have kids the same age and we are all just about the same age. They have all known each other either their entire lives or since college. They were all at Alabama when Jay was playing ball there. So I immediately hit it off with them.

Lisa isn't just my friend, she's also my decorator, and we joke that she's like my Mountain Brook manager, because she tells me what I need to remember and what's going on. "By the way, Audrey needs to do this . . . ," she'll say, or, "Don't forget that Olivia should do that . . . Did you send in the pictures for the senior thing?" Lisa knows how frazzled my life can get and how busy I can be. She's really funny, too, so she feeds my sense of humor.

Sullins is my practical, down-to-earth friend. She goes to bed at eightish every night. Though she's only a few years older than me, she seems like an older sister. She's like a sounding board because she listens to me. She thinks that she has the most boring life compared to me. I'll tell her these huge, dramatic things going on in my life and she'll respond with, "I had chicken for dinner last night." We laugh about that because it's pretty much true. Sullins is practically a professional tennis player and we play tennis a lot. She's an incredible decorator as well. Her husband is fourteen years older, and her life is just so different from mine. It's calm. And she brings a calm to my life.

Renee is the friend with whom I share a lot of personal values when it comes to being a mom and a wife. We both love to cook for our families, we are both servants at heart, and we are both traditional thinkers when it comes to marriage. She and I walk a lot, and these walks are like counseling sessions for both of us. We each have three kids exactly the same age.

Libba is fun and always laughing. She has triplets who are the same age as Olivia (we call her Livy) and a daughter the same age as Avery. Libba and I have a lot of great, deep talks. All of these gals have traveled with me a lot. I love to have girlfriends go on tour with me, they all know exactly what to do and how to be on the bus. It's a blast and they are so helpful—they will just jump in and start steaming my clothes or handing things to KK to help get me dressed. And we are laughing the whole time!

Chapter 12

THE PLANE CRASH

Sometimes life brings a new perspective through hard times or even terrifying experiences. I experienced this as a little girl when I survived being hit by a car. On December 7, 2012, I had another terrible perspective shift when the plane I was flying in nearly crashed. Things like that change you forever.

I had a one-off show up in Minnesota at a place in the middle of nowhere that was going to be hard to get to. I needed to fly from Birmingham to Atlanta, and then from Atlanta to a city in Minnesota where I'd meet KK and Matt and the rest of the band. Then we'd have to make a two-hour drive to the event.

Instead, I asked a friend who often flew me if he was available to fly us up to Minnesota and then back to Birmingham. He couldn't do it this time but recommended someone else. I wasn't thrilled by that idea, but he assured me, saying, "There are two pilots, and they're both incredible, been flying for years. You'll be in good hands."

I agreed to the idea and then called KK, saying, "Why don't you drive down to Birmingham and fly up with me? Then, after the show, we can all fly back together, and you and Matt can spend Sunday with Jay, the kids, and me. We'll make some food, hang out, have dinner."

I was excited about the plan, as I always am when family gets together. But this was an especially good time, too, because KK was six months pregnant with Milly.

KK agreed to the idea, and she and Matt drove down in time for us to fly out. On the plane, we met the two pilots. They were really nice and seemed experienced, and one of the pilots had brought his girlfriend along. He was probably in his sixties, and she was this upper-middle-aged, beautiful, classy southern woman. We had a great time talking with her as we flew up to Minnesota.

When we landed, my tour manager was there with a black SUV to take us all to the venue. It was a great show, and right after the meet and greet we headed back to the private airport. We brought our after-show food and drinks with us to have on the flight home. It was really cold and had been snowing, so we were excited to get on the plane and go!

For some reason, Matt thought it would be funny to film us boarding the plane. I heard him ask the pilots, "What kind of plane is this?" and KK and I were like, "What the heck are you doing? You don't film before a private plane ride, or take pictures! That's bad luck!" I mean, I fly a lot, and I fly private a lot, but I think everyone is a little nervous anytime they fly. It's just not the most comfortable thing in the world to do. I think most people would admit that flying causes a bit of anxiety. Since I had such bad PTSD from getting hit by a car and from my exhaustion breakdown in 2005, I always keep anti-anxiety meds with me, especially when I have to fly. I am terrified of having a panic attack on a plane. Or anytime.

We settled into our seats. Matt was sitting across from me and KK was beside me, so the seat beside Matt was empty. I remember telling Matt, "Hey, it might be a little bumpy for the first ten to twenty minutes or so, because we will be going through the clouds." I'm not sure why I said that to him, because he flies all the time. I think Matt and I have a bit of clairvoyance, because he predicted something bad was going to happen to me the day before I got hit by a car. For some reason, I felt like I needed to prepare him for something. And I felt responsible because I had arranged for the private jet.

He was like, "Okay, cool." This being December in Minnesota, it was not just cold but COLD. Cold and dark, and we were in the middle of nowhere. We said goodbye to my tour manager and shut the door. We took off, and right as we started to pour some glasses of wine, put our tray tables down, and open our food, the plane bounced. And then it bounced again, and again, and not just a turbulence bounce but a "something is wrong" bounce. At first we tried to shrug it off and convince ourselves it was in fact just turbulence. You know how you do that thing where everybody grabs their armrests and closes their eyes, thinking it's going to stop? But it didn't stop, and ten to fifteen seconds later we knew we were in real trouble.

We were literally bouncing all over the sky, and some kind of alarm started going off, and the pilot's girlfriend started yelling out his name. I thought, she flies with him five times a week, everywhere they go, and if she's screaming his name, then this is awful.

Across from me, Matt started freaking out, saying, "Oh God, Oh God, Oh Jesus, Jehovah." He was calling out for everyone, just in case.

I tried to stay calm for KK and my unborn niece and not do any damage to them by freaking out. But KK remained the most calm. It seemed her motherly instincts had kicked in. She was clinging to the armrests, saying, "It's okay, it's okay, Matt. It's okay."

Matt said, "No, it's not! We're crashing. Sara, we're crashing!"

I can't ever tell this part of the story without laughing at how my brother kept saying, "Sara, we're crashing!" I don't know if he said this because he and I have been best friends since we were little or if instead he was accusing me, like, "Sara, we're crashing, and you made me ride on this damn airplane!"

It was probably a little bit of both.

All of a sudden, I was thrown to the floor—I mean completely thrown down, head to the floor, at KK's feet. It was the strangest sensation to be stuck there, like a giant magnet was holding me down. I couldn't lift my head; I couldn't lift any part of me. I simply cannot describe to you the chaos that was happening. It was truly horrifying. When you're in a chaotic situation like that, seconds seem like hours, and it's excruciating. And your brain reacts oddly and slowly. Finally, I couldn't take it anymore, and I yelled to the pilots, "What the hell is going on?"

Matt yelled back, "We're crashing, we're crashing!" I don't think I had ever realized how redundant Matt can be. And negative, jeez . . . think on the bright side for a change.

My brother started to realize that he was passing out. Thank God he is a very smart man, because he also realized: If I'm passing out, the pilots might be, too! So he started yelling at them, "Hey! Don't pass out! Y'all, DO NOT PASS OUT!!!" When I heard that, I forced my head to look up at the pilots, and they were both slinking down in their chairs. They were indeed fighting passing out.

Matt kept screaming to them and told the pilot's girlfriend to keep them awake. She was banging on their chairs, shouting, "Don't pass out, y'all!"—and this seemed to be working. They did this thing that they learned in training where you do a major sit-up and clench your stomach muscles. It's a technique Air Force pilots use to keep from passing out when they're pulling g's—feeling the effects of g-forces. It works.

At some point during all of this I realized that we were crashing (I hate it when Matt is right), and I knew we had not been in the air long, so we were probably seconds from dying. I completely accepted it. It was so strange and peaceful. My fear subsided, and all I could think about was: I'm about to be face-to-face with Jesus. It's actually happening, and I'm going to meet my heavenly Father. I know that sounds crazy, but it's absolutely true.

Finally, it stopped being chaotic, and everything became dead silent. Nobody talked or moved. The copilot turned around, and all he said was, "We're okay now."

Matt looked out the window and said, "We're not okay." Damn it, Matt!

The left wing had crumpled up like a Coke can because of the pressure.

The copilot called back, "We're going to make an emergency landing in Fargo, North Dakota. We'll be on the ground in about twenty minutes."

Suddenly, I felt really scared. The pilot's girlfriend moved back and sat with us, and we all huddled together and sobbed for the next twenty minutes, saying "Are you okay?" "Yes, are you?" "Yes, thank God, oh thank you, God!"

As relieved as I was, those last twenty minutes before we landed were torturous. My emotions were about to be out of control because I had just accepted death, and now that we were okay, I started to panic because all I wanted was to be with my children and husband. That twenty minutes seemed like a lifetime.

As the plane hit the runway in Fargo, there were police and emergency vehicles waiting for us.

I called Jay before the plane had stopped.

"Why are you calling me?!" he asked in a worried tone. He knew I should not be calling him yet because it was supposed to be a two-hour flight and I was calling him forty-five minutes after I'd already texted that we were in the air, so it freaked him out. "We had a problem with our plane and had to make an emergency landing," I said as calmly as possible.

"What happened, baby?" He sounded very scared.

"I'm not exactly sure, something broke or went terribly wrong. I'll call you back as soon as we talk to the pilots."

It was hard for him to let me off the phone, because he wanted all the details, but I didn't have any yet. I promised to call him back as soon as I could and assured him that I was fine. Matt was calling the band and crew, and KK was calling her mom. Everyone was shocked at our news.

Then I called my mom. When I heard her voice, I started bawling. You know what I mean? Something about hearing your mom's voice when you're scared or stressed is just so comforting. When I called her after my anxiety attack, same thing. It scared her, of course, but she kept her voice steady. "Well, I'm so glad you're okay, honey. I know that had to be terrifying, but it's all over and you're okay now . . ." All the comforting things that you would want your mom to say.

Once everything calmed down and we were all wrapped in blankets and had coffee in our hands waiting for our ride to the hotel, the pilots started telling us what the hell had happened. They took off on manual mode, and then when we were around 10,000 feet, they switched to autopilot. At that moment our plane went crazy. They realized later that the gyroscope had gone out. The gyroscope is the piece of equipment that tells the plane if it is right side up or upside down. Because it wasn't working properly, as soon as they switched to autopilot the plane automatically turned upside down and started plummeting toward the ground. And the whole time, we never knew that we were upside down. Interesting fact, our wine never spilled! That was the biggest blessing of all. These two pilots really and truly saved our lives because they were so well trained that they were able to get us out of what was probably the most precarious flying situation they'd ever been in. They both stayed calm.

The copilot had spent many years of his career doing aerobatic shows, so he had a real sense of how to "feel" what was happening. You have to remember that we were in the clouds and in the dark; no one could see anything. When the plane was screaming at them and all their control panels were telling them that we were about a second from the ground, they took a chance and pulled up. There was a 50-50 chance that they would make the right decision. They did something that's called a split S maneuver to get us headed straight back up toward the sky. Remember when I said I had been thrown to the floor and couldn't lift my head? That was because of the g-force. When we were pulling up, it actually gave the sensation of being pulled down. We pulled 4.5 g's to get back up, and that's what caused the wing to crumple. A plane like that is not designed to pull that many g's. Neither am I.

Our tour manager had been on the phone arranging a car service to take us to a hotel in Fargo. Of all the nights, there had been some big game or event happening, and almost every hotel was sold out. The only place that had any rooms was the Howard Johnson's. We were so tired and in need of warmth and comfort that we didn't care where we stayed. "Just book it!" I said. Well, that was a big mistake. They only had two rooms, so Matt and KK and I shared a room, and the two pilots and the girlfriend shared a room. I have no idea what in the world was happening, but when we walked into the Howard Johnson's, it was packed! People were everywhere, and they had been partying like rock stars. They were yelling and dancing and acting insane right there in the lobby, which was connected to a bar area. It was so scary it made the "plane crash" seem like a Sunday afternoon drive in the country! Then I had a terrifying thought: "Wait, maybe we did die, and we are in HELL!"

The next day, some friends of ours in Birmingham sent an airplane up to Fargo to bring us home. It was the exact same type of airplane as the other one. Thankfully, it was a beautiful, sunny day, with clear blue skies, and we told ourselves that we'd be fine. I mean, what were the chances of anything like that ever happening again? And I just wanted to get home so badly.

Before we boarded, the new pilot could see that I was nervous. He said, "I had a perfect and easy flight up here, and I will fly on manual all the way home. Don't worry about anything. You'll be home before you know it." I was so touched that he took that moment to say that to me. One time I heard a sermon by Matt Chandler, one of my all-time favorite preachers in the world, and he said, "Never pass up a moment to say something kind to someone. If it pops into your head, then say it, especially if it would make someone feel good." I love that. I try to do that always.

Before we left, I called my assistant at the time and asked her to go to the grocery store and get steaks and wine and cheese and desserts and everything yummy she could think of. I invited some friends and family members over to just spend the evening TOGETHER. I wanted people around me to celebrate that we survived.

I didn't realize what would happen when I got home, though. As soon as I walked in and saw my babies, I just about fell apart. Just seeing them made it all too real. What if I had died? What if I had left those three precious people motherless? I hugged them so tightly and then said, "I'm going to go take a quick shower. I'm disgusting, you guys!" I was trying to keep a smile on my face as I sort of backed out of the living room so they wouldn't see me burst into tears. And boy, did I. I got in that shower and sobbed and sobbed and sobbed. I think I was just trying to stay strong until we were home. Not that I didn't already realize it, but it hit me again that I love those three human beings so much that it scares me sometimes. All you moms are shaking your heads YES right now.

Jay stood in the doorway to my bathroom and said, "Baby, are you okay?" I stepped out of the shower and wrapped a robe around myself and just fell into his arms. Jay is the perfect person to hug when you need it. He is huge and his big, muscular arms can make me feel so safe and loved. I pulled on some sweats and Uggs and a big, warm sweater and with no makeup and wet hair joined everyone in the kitchen for a night of food, drink, and gratitude to God for saving us.

It was so hard to let Matt and KK leave and go back to Nashville the next day. We were traumatized, there was no doubt about it, and the six of us who were on that plane are the only people on this earth who understand it completely. I felt like if Matt and KK left, then I would be alone with my PTSD with no one to talk to about it. I went into sort of a depression for a few weeks, and we had a group text among the six of us that was very helpful. We texted every day during that time. And still every year on December 7 we text one another.

There were actually seven of us who survived. My sweet niece Milly was born the following March 17. A St. Patrick's Day baby. She's about to turn six and she is absolutely the reason God saved that plane from going down, because she needed to be born. And guess what? She became a big sister in August 2019. Isn't life just amazing?

Even though my kids aren't being raised the same way I was, meaning working on a farm outside of a small town, I'm teaching them to work hard and take pride in everything they do, to find moderation in life, to love and be loyal to family, to be honest, be a good friend, and find God.

What we experience as children creates memories, beliefs, habits, and also some pain that remains with us our entire lives. Childhood pain shaped me in a lot of ways! My parents' divorce and a near crippling accident, growing up performing on stage, and many other things made me the woman I am today. Every experience teaches us something, and that's what I love about life.

PART TWO

Now

Chapter 13

MARRIED WITH CHILDREN

J ay and I started our marriage with seven children, and because of that, we knew we needed to set aside time to be together. Our work schedules made that challenging enough, but when you add seven kids to the mix, it takes some work. But it's never seemed like work. We have always been such a great team, we just make things happen. Jay is very paternal; parenting comes easy to him. There have been many times when he has loaded up all seven kiddos and taken them to an Alabama game or to a movie. We have been on a lot of vacations with all nine of us, and we have taken the kids on the bus plenty of times.

It's like we are a tag-team wrestling couple. We both know exactly when to step in and help the other one. We believe in family and kids first above everything. The one thing we have always done, however, is that once we put the kids to bed, we tell them, "That's it, kitchen closed, and parents are off the clock." Not that any of them ever obeyed this completely, but we tried. Almost every night since we've been married, we sit outside together for an hour or two and just talk. Or watch something on the outside TV. I can't really remember how this routine started, but it works great for us. I think we go outside because we really feel "away" from the kids. We know they can't hear us talking, and we can't hear them playing or whatever. We used to say, "Blood or bones—don't interrupt us unless you see blood or bones!" Obviously we were joking. The best is when we are on vacation in a rental house and they don't know where we are sitting outside. We have laughed a lot watching them walk around looking for us. Again, exaggerating. Gosh.

It's not always easy finding that balance. Plenty of parents live their lives around their kids' extracurricular activities, and we have done that, too. We never wanted to miss one single game or school play or anything they did. One year Avery, Braxton, Harrison, Sarah Ashlee, Olivia, and Audrey were all playing baseball/softball. It was ridiculous. I think we counted that we went to twenty-something games one weekend. But it was worth it, and I would do it all over again if I absolutely HAD to and could get paid for it.

Jay and I are both really chill people and parents. We expect our kids to be respectful, and we make it very clear that we want them to represent God, themselves, and our family in an upstanding way. But we don't freak out. I do not yell at my kids. My parenting style has always been to respect my kids as human beings. I don't think you should ever be afraid of your parents. You should fear and respect them but not be AFRAID of them. There's a big difference. I really believe that most of the time the mother sets the tone in the home. Dads can, too, but it's usually the mom who decides if it's going to be a good day or a stressful day. When a mom gets overwhelmed with too much housework and not enough time in the day, she can really make life miserable for everyone else in the home.

That's why it's important to have good communication, not just in your marriage but in your family. If I'm feeling overwhelmed or exhausted, I always tell my family what's going on so they know what to expect. I am always amazed at how many women expect their husbands to just "know" what they want. Men are not wired to see the same things women see. When I walk through my house, I see every little thing that is out of order or dusty, and anything that needs to be done. It's impossible for me to walk by a towel on the floor without either picking it up or at least being bothered by it. If I put something in the trash and realize it's full and nothing else will fit in it, I have to pull it out and put in a new bag. But kids and men don't see that stuff. They just don't care the way that moms do. And it's likely never going to change.

There's no point in getting mad at your family. Just tell them what you need. I tell my girls every single day to "go to Atlanta." Atlanta stands for ATL, and ATL means ADVANCE THE LAUNDRY. Every time they think of it, they need to do one thing to help me with the laundry. If there are clothes in the washer, put them in the dryer, and if the dryer is full, take the clothes out and fold them. This is not something that they like to do or remember to do, but they will do it when I remind them. Jay always tells me, "Don't expect me to read your mind, and don't get mad at me for not doing something that you didn't ask me to do, because I'm never going to see the things you see, so just ask me to help and I'll help." So many women stay quiet and stew inside. He didn't get the hints she was putting out there, and then he says, "Is something wrong?"

And she says, "No, why?"

"Because you seem upset about something."

"No, not upset about anything." (Except that you walked right by the trash and didn't take it out. Same with the sink full of dishes. And no one in this house EVER feeds the dogs but me, and am I the ONLY one with working arms to fold laundry?) "Nothing's wrong... good night."

It's much kinder and wiser to just speak what's on your mind, before you get angry. Even if you have to say it many, many, many times. I think all moms who have sons would agree that we wouldn't want our future daughters-in-law to talk to our sons the way we sometimes talk to our husbands.

That doesn't let men off the hook. I think men could do a better job or make a better effort at trying to know what we need. I see a lot of men who are clueless when it comes to being aware of what all needs to be done. Women are such multitaskers, and we can get a million things done in one day, and men are just not as much that way. I think men are more goal-oriented or task-oriented and think in a "one thing at a time" way. Men can compartmentalize, which is a great gift. Women put everything that's going on in the world together in one big ball. This is how women think: "Oh my gosh, I have so much going on, and on top of that, my friend was mean to me yesterday, and how am I going to handle that when I'm so fat today? Not to mention that my daughter has a game tonight, so when will I have time to make dinner, since there is so much laundry to do, and I have to call my mom, and what about the wall? There's so much fighting going on about immigration, and that just makes me stressed, so all I want to do is eat ice cream and read, but I'm worried that the place we want to rent for our vacation isn't going to be available at the time we need it, so I better make sure I get the oil changed in my car..."

That is how women are tortured on the daily. And this is most men . . .

"I know I have a lot to do, and we are having money problems, but I'm not going to think about that right now because the game is on."

Honest to God, I remember one of my friends telling me once that her husband said he couldn't do something she had asked him to do because "I had to watch the baby . . ." And I really don't think he was being lazy; he meant that sincerely. "I'll have to do that tomorrow because I'm watching the baby today." And fathers are great at playing with the kids. I've always admired that in men, how they can play and play and play and give the child hours of undivided attention in that way. Moms don't play. Ask any mom if she enjoys sitting down and playing with the Barbie dolls, or any form of "pretend" with her kids. If she's honest she will say no, because she feels like there's something else she should be doing. Like laundry or dishes or cleaning the house or paying bills. "I don't have time to sit down and play pretend, are you kidding me?"

Because, let's be honest, women LOVE to worry. It's what we do best. And it's really not what God wants for us, because He loves us so much and wants us to have peace and joy. True peace that comes from knowing that He is in control and cares about our daily needs. Would any of us GOOD parents ever just ignore our children if they were hurting or in need of something? No. And neither does God. He is always providing and protecting.

Like my mother, Jay is great at talking me off the ledge. He's able to hear all of my worries and explain to me how everything is going to work out and be fine. He likes to help me fix things. I don't know why women complain about their husbands wanting to fix things: "He always tries to fix my problems, when really all I need him to do is listen." No, I would rather someone fix my problems for me, thank you very much! If we just want someone to vent to, that's a girlfriend. If we want someone to take action on our behalf or offer advice on how to fix the problem, that's your husband.

I love that book *The 5 Love Languages*. I think that theory is brilliant. Everyone has different things that make them feel loved, or feel like they are giving love. It's SO important to know what those are, and to tell your loved ones. In particular your spouse. My number one love language is acts of service. Hands down. If you do something for me to take the burden off me, I feel so loved. And that's how I show love. I have a true servant's heart. I love to make food, fill plates for people, bring drinks, give you a blanket, bring you a warm towel after a shower, clean your room for you, get you a glass of water to take to bed . . . I should have gone into the food and beverage or hotel industry.

My second love language is quality time. If you take the time to really be present when you're with me, or want to spend time with me, that makes me feel loved. Ask anyone in my family what makes me the most angry. They will all immediately say, "if we are on our phones while Mom is talking to us or wanting our attention."

My third love language is words of affirmation. I mean, I perform for a living. I require praise. So I do feel really loved when someone says, "Good job!"

∞

I think the keys to having a great marriage and great relationships are pretty simple and commonsense. Just be a good person. Don't be a bitch and don't be a bastard. Have respect for one another, but understand that respect is earned, not given. Help each other out; don't be selfish. Don't be stubborn. Smile a lot, and always ask yourself if what you're about to say is going to help or hurt the day. Don't try to be right all the time and win every argument, and stop being so defensive! No one likes an overly defensive person. They are really annoying. And stop being so sensitive. Give each other the benefit of the doubt. Maybe someone didn't mean anything by a look or a non-response to your comment. Don't be too needy or clingy. Have your own friends and things that you do that are separate from your spouse.

And SHARE! Share time and attention and household needs. Don't always leave it to him to take out the trash, and don't always leave it to her to make the bed. Don't ever be lazy with your marriage. It can slip away from you if you're not careful, and it's not always easy to get it back. Cherish and nurture the "it" factor that was there in the beginning. It's important to maintain some level of mystery and independence from your spouse. After twenty years, she can still say, "There's just something so cool about my husband that leaves me wondering what makes him tick. What is he thinking?" Or, "I'll never fully understand my wife, but she is the sexiest woman I've ever met and I'm just in awe of her every day." And, y'all, this will not happen if you're not kind. If you are not treating your spouse with kindness and respect, he or she won't look at you that way, ever. You will just be a burden.

And for God's sake, whenever possible, have separate bathrooms.

Chapter 14

RAISE THEM UP

One of the best compliments I can ever receive is when someone tells me what great kids I have. You will see this huge smile come over my face. When I decided to have my first child, ever the perfectionist that I am, I knew that I would pour my whole heart and life into that child and sacrifice anything for him or her. Yes, I waited all three times until they were born to find out what I was having! Almost no one does that these days. I don't know why I'm so old-fashioned about some things, but I just thought that would be fun, and I wanted to wait and meet this person who was alive inside me and discover who they were when I first laid eyes on them. I have to say, if you're inclined at all to wait till they're born to find out what you're having, it's REALLY fun! Being a mom has been my greatest joy in life.

Being pregnant? Um . . . no. I'm sorry, but pregnancy is the worst.

I hate those women who don't get sick and don't gain extra weight and talk about how they just "love being pregnant." Whatever! Either they are lying or they are aliens. The main reason that pregnancy is nearly intolerable is the nausea. I can't even describe it. It's having the stomach flu for months and months. I was sick all the way through the sixth month at least. And it's not just regular nausea—it NEVER stops. I would think for about five minutes, Oh, maybe it's going away! And then I would see a branch blow in the wind, and that would make it come back. I hated my house and everything in it, and every smell in the world. There was no soap, no lotion, no candle, no food, no flower, nothing that wouldn't make me feel sick. I begged and pleaded with my ob-gyn, "Isn't there anything you can give me? This can't be right! Is there a gremlin living inside me?" She just kind of laughed and said, "You can try ginger." WTH? I was like, "What's her number? I'll call her right now!"

Oh, I tried ginger, I tried crackers, I tried Sprite, I tried eating, I tried not eating, I tried sleeping, I tried praying. Nothing worked. I remember one day I decided to take a warm bath to soothe myself, and I sat there and sobbed and begged God to take my nausea away, but He chose not to answer that particular prayer. To this day I cannot have ginger because it reminds me of pregnancy nausea. And I am not a cute pregnant person. I don't know what it is, but I get instantly ghoulish. I don't "glow." I get so mad when they portray pregnant women on TV shows or in movies and they have super-skinny arms and legs with just a perfect little belly. That is NOT reality. I gain fifteen pounds every time I have PMS, so pregnancy is just that times a million. Everything is odd—my skin goes crazy, my hair turned gray, I got that pregnancy mask, I got fat, my feet swelled to the point that I became a hobbit, and I was a bitch. A nauseous bitch who cried all the time.

BUT . . . when I went to get my first sonogram and heard the baby's heartbeat, I thought, this is worth everything I'm going through and more. Then at the twenty-week visit, when I got to actually see the baby on the ultrasound and take a picture home with me, I was the happiest person in the whole wide world. I stared at that picture every day until he was born. On August 21, 1999, I gave birth to my son, Avery Jack. Well, as much as I just loved being pregnant, I really was stressing about having the baby and losing the weight. I knew that I would be performing at the CMA Awards in September, and I'd heard that a lot of first-time pregnancies can go past the due date. I don't know what I was worried about, though. I only gained fifty pounds. Surely I could lose that in five weeks. So we scheduled an induction on August 20.

They wanted me to come in that morning and get all hooked up. I thought, this is so great, I'll be home by tomorrow afternoon. Best-laid plans. My mom and stepdad came down to Nashville, my sister Ashley was living there and so was Matt, so I had a decent amount of family support. Everyone went with us to the hospital and waited. And waited. And waited. One thing they didn't tell me was that sometimes when they induce labor, and the contractions start and you feel like you might die, some people want an epidural. That's a big huge needle that they put in your spine to numb you so you can get through the labor without screaming bloody murder and ruining your precious vocal chords that you're totally going to need to support the baby you're about to have.

Well, in order to put that foot-long needle ever so delicately between the bones of your spine so as not to paralyze you, they have to dial back the medicine that made you start labor in the first place. "Okay, that sounds good," I said. Soon, an anesthesiologist came in and said, "I'm going to need you to turn over on your side. I'm going to paint this orange stuff all over your ass, and then you're going to feel a stick. Please try your hardest not to move or breathe."

Again, "okay" was all I could say. I was terrified, but even more scared of having another one of those hateful contractions. So I turned over like a beached whale, and I could feel him move my hospital gown so my entire backside was exposed, and then the unthinkable happened. He said, "I know your guitar player."

WHAT!!!!!!!!!!!!

"Oh, you do? That's cool, he's a great guy," I managed to say. "Yeah, we are in the same church group," blah, blah, blah. I could have died of embarrassment right there. I was so mortified, I almost said, "You know what? I don't even feel any pain—I don't need the epidural after all." And, "Get your hands off my ass and your needle out of my spine if you KNOW who I am!" All I could think about was him telling people, "I know I can't tell you who, but I did an epidural on a certain country music star, her name rhymes with Cara Blevins . . . And, man oh man, you should have seen how much weight she's gained!"

Thankfully for his sake, the shot worked, and all of a sudden I was in heaven! The pain was gone, and I was warm and comfortable. Now all I would have to do was lie there and wait for them to say, "Okay, Sara, it's time to push." Nope. I lay there that whole night (fighting panic and anxiety from memories of being confined to a hospital bed) and the next morning until finally my doctor came in and said, "I think we are going to need to do a C-section because you aren't progressing at all, and every time you have a contraction now, the baby's heart rate is starting to drop."

I was like, "Hell yes, let's get that ball rolling and get this baby OUT of me!" I could tell I wasn't progressing and I was only dilated to five centimeters, so if it wasn't for the miracle of C-section surgeries, I could have lain there and died trying to get the baby out.

They started prepping the operating room, and me, and wheeled me down the hall. I was nervous, but I trusted my ob-gyn immensely and I knew this was the right decision. When they got me in the room, they started putting all this warm stuff all over my body, kind of like heavy heating pads, and my doctor said, "Sara, can you feel this?"

"I don't feel anything," I said. And she said, "Good, because I was just pinching your skin really hard with forceps." So having the assurance that I was totally numb, she started cutting, and telling me exactly what she was doing with each step. Then less than ten minutes later she said, "And now we are going to bring your baby out. Are you ready?"

"Yes!" I sobbed. And this moment will forever be etched in my mind's eye till the day I die, and probably even when I'm in heaven. I felt this enormous amount of pressure as they pulled my baby out and said, "It's a boy!" The doctor held him up high with his face pointed toward me, and I had never, ever, ever seen anything more beautiful or miraculous in my life.

My son. My firstborn. He cried instantly. Right then when she held him up for me to see, he cried. I wanted to hold him so badly, but they told me they needed to do just a few routine checks and then they would bring him right over. About one minute later as my doctor was closing me up, the most excruciating pain came over my left side just below my collarbone. I screamed out in horror, not knowing what in the world could possibly be causing me that kind of pain, and so close to my heart. The last thing I remember was the nurse holding that breathing thing that puts you to sleep over my mouth, and I was out like a light.

I think I was unconscious for about thirty to forty-five minutes. When I woke up, my mom was standing right beside me, holding my

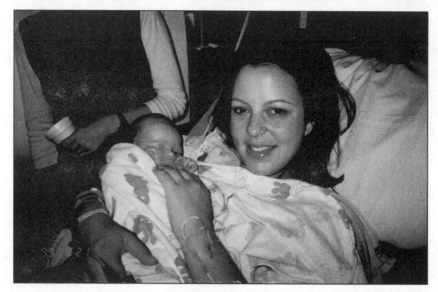

Avery Jack

hand. "You have a beautiful baby boy, Saree." (That's her nickname for me.)

"Is he okay? Is everything okay?" I cried.

She said, "Yes, he is fine. They are getting him now. We just watched him get all of his shots, and he's healthy and perfect and so cute."

"What happened to me?" I asked. She said she didn't know, and that the doctors didn't really, either. She told me the reason they put me under was in case something really was wrong and the epidural was wearing off. I needed to be asleep while they figured out and fixed whatever might be wrong. To this day, I have no idea what that pain was. The doctor's best guess was that when she was putting me all back together, she hit a nerve that caused the pain. But there was nothing at all wrong with my heart or any part of me, for that matter.

FINALLY, they brought me my baby. I simply could not believe it. I was in awe of him. He was an angel, a true gift from God. I was so thankful and humbled that my heavenly Father was entrusting me with this human being. I will say, all three times I have given birth were the happiest days of my life. I loved those days in the hospital. I love the drugs, the nurses, the middle-of-the-night visits when they wake you so you can feed your baby—all of it. I think it would be an amazing thing to be a neonatal nurse or a nurse who takes care of the new mommies. No matter how tired I was, I was so excited every time they brought my baby in for a feeding. It was like Christmas morning each time.

It's crazy, too, how you completely memorize their faces right when they are born. I know they have to for security, but when they would bring him in and check my wristband to make sure it matched his, I would always think, "There's no way I wouldn't know him. Already, I have him memorized."

I spent five glorious days in the hospital learning how to be a mom. How to change him, swaddle him, and feed him. But then it was time to go home. I honestly think I forgot about that part. I remember thinking, "Take him home? Is one of these nurses coming home with me? Because I don't remember anything they taught me over the last five days!" And then when I realized that we were going to have to put this precious angel in a car and drive home through other moving cars? Every ounce of my "mother bear" instincts immediately showed up. I, of course, sat in the back of our SUV, right next to Avery, and I watched everything like a hawk—every car that came anywhere near us. Mercifully, we made it home, and just as I'd settled down on the couch, my mom called. And once again, as soon as I heard her voice, I started bawling. "I don't know what I'm doing! What if I mess up?" She said, "You'll be fine. He's your baby and you know what to do. Take it one day at a time and call me if you have any questions, day or night." And she was right. Those first few weeks were exhausting and scary at times, but I eventually fell right into it and enjoyed every minute of it.

I won't bore you with all the details of my girls' births, but I had scheduled C-sections with both of them. Each went very smoothly. When Olivia was born, I couldn't believe she was a girl. I waited three years after Avery to have her and had been solely focused on boy stuff, so I think I just assumed I would have another boy.

My doctor held her up high for me to see and said, "It's a girl!" I was shocked and so excited that God gave me a daughter. Olivia Margaret, eight pounds, seven ounces. Almost the next day, her eyes turned dark brown, and she was the most beautiful, precious thing I'd ever seen. She was such a quiet, pensive baby. She would just stare at you with those big brown eyes, and you could tell she was intensely thinking about something. And then when she was just twenty months old, Audrey Elizabeth was born. Audrey was a surprise, and when I found out I was pregnant with her, we had just released "Back Seat of a Greyhound Bus" as a single. I was very stressed out because I didn't think I was ready to go through another pregnancy so soon. I tried to be positive and say, "You never know, maybe I won't be sick this time." I was. But I made it through the pregnancy somehow and again chose not to find out what I was having until the birth. This time I had a different doctor because my ob-gyn was also in the hospital at the same time, having her baby. We scheduled a C-section on October 4, and by 10:00 a.m., they were holding up my third child. They pointed her toward me and said, "Sara, you have another beautiful baby girl." Avery was five years old now, and he was praying the whole time for a little brother. Not that he didn't absolutely adore Olivia, but he just wanted a brother so badly. As they were rolling me back into my room, Avery was in there with my mom waiting, and

Not many people know that I'm a drummer!

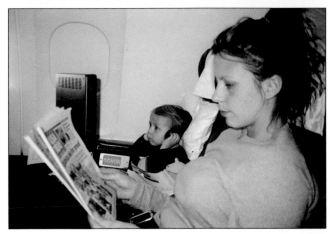

Avery and me on our way to Switzerland

Brenner, Gary Gilbert, and me on the set of the "Born to Fly" music video

Rocking the retro vibe when
I first got signed to RCA

Jay joining me
onstage at CMA Fest

My beautiful mother

Signing with my idol Reba on the Girls' Night Out Tour

One of my first professional headshots

The mandolin was bigger than I was!

The Barker Bunch

In my element in the
recording studio

Winning ACM Top Female Vocalist
is one of my life highlights

Kaelin (KK), me, and Craig Dunn a the NAB Awards in Washington, D.C.

Olivia and me in the recording studio

My dad, Jack Evans

Olivia and me in a
dressing room/locker
room before singing the
National Anthem

Avery, me, my dad,
and Grandma

Holding Audrey a few days
after she was born

Avery's first Christmas

My mom, me, and Melvin on the
tour bus at the CMA Awards

We loved our animals
on the farm! Me, Matt,
Lesley, and Ashley.

Behind the scenes on the set of my "Suds in the Bucket" music video (secretly pregnant with Olivia)

My sweet Granny and Papa

I said, "Avery, you have another little sister!" And he put both hands on his head and said, "Oh no!!!!!!" Poor baby. I wanted to cry for him. But I knew that he would fall in love with his new baby sister as soon as he met her. And he did.

All three of my children are very close. They've been through a lot together. That's how siblings are. They have this bond, this knowing, that no one else, not even the parents, can be in on. It's just between them. And if you raise your kids right, they will be close their whole lives. All siblings fight from time to time, but I have only ever let it go so far without intervening. I try to be a mediator and get them to talk it out. My favorite thing is when a fight breaks out and it turns into a one- to two-hour-long talk between my kids and me. I like to keep them talking until they open up about what's really bothering them. It's usually hardest on whichever person is in the hot seat that particular time. I've been in the hot seat and it's not fun, but it's so good for us to TALK. Really talk, even if it's difficult or painful at times. Not only my three kids but *my three kids and I* are extremely close. The four of us have traveled together so much and have been through a lot together. I honestly am more proud of those three human beings than I am of anything I have ever done.

I worked really hard to develop their little personalities when they were toddlers. I made a nonstop effort to show them how to be great people. Teaching them to say "please" and "thank you," to push in their chair and throw away their trash—all of these little things add up to big ways to shape a child. Discipline is so important. I won't even talk about millennials. Eyes-rolling emoji. It's just unbelievable to me what is going on in some parts of the country, and some of the crazy ways in which people think. Social media and iPhones and Snapchat and all the other stuff are things I could write a whole different book about.

But I digress. I believe in disciplining children. It's so important. Beyond important. And it's for them. Not you. Them. It's hard to do. So many parents act like they are scared of their kids. Scared to make them upset or break their little hearts by taking something away from them when they've behaved badly. I've seen parents who let their kids scream at them or hit them! And these parents laugh it off or just tell them to stop, but they don't enforce the rules, and there aren't any real repercussions for bad behavior. To me, this is child abuse. To have children and then not teach them how to behave and how to have good manners and be respectful to you and other adults, and other people of all ages, for that matter. When you teach a child that the world revolves around her, you are hurting her. People don't like brats. They don't like them when they are little and still cute, and they especially don't like adult brats. So all you're doing when you refuse to discipline is ensuring that your precious child will have a hard time in life and in relationships.

Why would any loving parent do that? Because they are being selfish, in my opinion. They are being lazy and parenting in ways that make THEM feel good. Like letting your child play Xbox all day. Why do some parents do this? Because it's easier than making them stop. The child is going to throw a fit and beg to keep playing, and this means you have to get off the couch and "deal" with your child. It's much, much easier to let them do what they want. I have to constantly monitor phone use and time spent on Snapchat and Instagram and YouTube because children don't have a governor when it comes to this. It's all so addictive, so my job as the mom is to put limits on things. Create boundaries, draw lines in the sand, give rules. This is what parents are supposed to do. And when kids are little, they are going to cry. So let them cry. You're doing your JOB! They will thank you for it later. When you don't push back on a child who's being willful or disrespectful, they sense that you don't really care. And that is heartbreaking.

It isn't just the discipline that's important. It's crucial to pray for them and with them. Help them get to a place where they have a repentant heart. Teach your children how to apologize when they've done something wrong. Show them how to pray for forgiveness and ask for forgiveness from their parents. I always tell my kids I forgive them. I say I love them no matter what. Even more important, I apologize to my kids when I've done something wrong to them. When I've lost my temper or betrayed their trust, or have been too critical and I see that I've hurt them, I always say I'm sorry and ask for their forgiveness.

There is no getting around it. Your children are going to be disobedient and try to do things that are wrong. It's not their fault, it's their nature. Your job as a parent is to guide them through discipline and teach them how to tell right from wrong, how to develop kindness and recognize cruelty, how to learn consideration and give up selfishness. Usually a bad kid is a product of bad parenting. Like I always tell my kids, if there's a bully or a mean girl at school, it's usually because there's something going on at home for that child. They are hurting somehow and they need to hurt others. Or they are learning how to hurt others.

When a man abuses his wife, almost always he saw abuse in his home. It's not an excuse, but children learn what they see. You can't tell your kids to be good when they see you being bad. If you are at home and you're saying horrible things about someone and your kids are listening, they will do the same thing. If you and your spouse fight in front of your kids, you are changing who they are as people. Parents, being blessed with a child is exactly that: a blessing. A gift. And we should treasure this and work every single day to put all our effort into teaching them the direction they should go.

Sometimes kids aren't behaving, or they're acting angry because there's something happening inside of them. Maybe they feel ignored, or someone has hurt their feelings or scared them. Some behavior changes are just testing boundaries. Other times it's a cry for help. Things can get so busy it's easy for days to pass without really connecting or paying attention to this. Stop and pay attention. It matters!

Whether we like it or not, everything we do is passing on behaviors, values, and morals (for good or for bad) to our children. We've all heard it said that kids are like sponges soaking up the world. They are watching, listening to, and learning from you and the people they are around. From your example, they are figuring out how to be in the world. Who they will become has a lot to do with who you and your husband and the people you hang out with are.

One of the things I value is hard work. Working hard was bred into me by growing up on a farm. I am still intentional about passing on to my kids the importance of working hard at whatever they are doing. If it's sports, a school play, homework, or even keeping their rooms clean, I expect them to work hard.

I believe people should work hard in *every* area of life, and I have no tolerance for people giving up and not trying to be the very best they can be. My kids see how hard Jay and I work on a constant basis. We live it, and we expect it.

I detest laziness of any kind. I think it's a sin and a waste of life and possibilities. I'm a stickler for keeping a very neat house and car. I think if you get up every day and make your bed and do an overall cleaning of your house, you will be a much happier and more successful person. I can't function if my bed isn't made or if there are dirty dishes in the sink. Also, my rule is to ALWAYS carry in trash from the car. And keep your room and your own space clean. My kids really do this, too. Avery tells me that he feels he has to keep his house in

Nashville clean, and that he's glad I taught them this because it's helpful in being organized and getting things accomplished. I also taught my kids to always offer guests something to eat or drink, no matter what, anytime they have friends over. I am astonished at how many parents don't teach their kids basic manners. It's a tragedy. It's already hard enough to even get people to look at you and listen to you when you talk because everyone is on their freaking phones all the time, so you have to really work hard to instill good manners in your children.

One thing I've always done is tuck my kids in at bedtime. The routines changed over the years, but no matter what, I always go to their rooms, and usually Jay comes with me, and he will say a quick "night, love y'all." But I stay and wait until they are in the bed with blankets up around them. Sometimes I'll come in and start picking up clothes off the floor and we talk while I'm doing this. I think it's so comforting for a child to be "put to bed" instead of just saying good night from the couch where you are watching TV. I never want my girls to go to their rooms alone and put themselves to bed without me connecting with them and making sure they are happy and there is nothing in their hearts or on their minds that I need to help them with. Right up until Avery graduated and moved out, even though he would be up so late every night playing guitar, I would still go up to the playroom where all his gear was set up and where he spent almost all of his time practicing. I would always go in, sit down, and listen to him play for a while and talk to him before I went to tuck the girls in. I just have to say good night and I love you to them.

When all seven kids were little and Jay's kids would be here for the weekend or their different times in the summer, we would have these big, fun rituals at night. We went through a phase where Jay would put on a puppet show for them while they all sat cross-legged on the bed. Then we would take the boys to their room and tuck them in and pray over them, then go to the girls' room and pray over them and tuck them in.

So much has changed. Three of our children are out of the home now, and the rest are teenagers. Life moves at such a fast pace, and you have to make sure that every moment counts. Especially while your kids are growing up. People used to tell me all the time, "Boy, it sure goes by fast." And I used to think they were exaggerating or something, but I'm here to tell you, it goes by fast. Much faster than I want it to. But we can't do a damn thing about it except enjoy the ride and make life as perfect as we can.

As I said before, if I could be anyone I wanted to be for a day, I would be each of my children. I want to know what they think of me. What they think of Jay, how they see our marriage and our dynamic. I want to know how they really feel. Do they feel loved? Do they feel criticized? How am I doing as a mom? How do they really feel about life and their future and their past? What are they most afraid of or sad about? What do they worry about? What are they really excited about or dreaming of?

Another key component of child-rearing is a sense of humor. I am grateful that our mom raised us with humor. It can be used in so many ways. If there's something you need to address that you're cringing over, just be funny about it. Teach your children not to be too serious about life. Life is meant to be lived and enjoyed, and laughter is the best medicine for any ailment. Laughter releases endorphins and makes everything better. My favorite thing is to tell a funny story and hold everyone in the room captive with it. I love to exaggerate and be over-the-top when I'm imitating someone. Another one of my specialties is taking something funny, or a joke, or something we are teasing someone about, and running it into the ground. Some things that are funny get funnier and funnier if said over and over again.

When I was in third grade, my mom decided that I should be a gas pump for Halloween. I actually did not think this was funny at all—I wanted to be something that all of my girlfriends were going to be, like Cinderella, or Pocahontas, or a baby doll. But nope, my mom thought it would be hilarious to make me a gas pump. (Now that I think about it, I bet she didn't have money to buy me a costume.) First she got this huge box and put it on me. I just stood there in the dark wondering how in the world this costume would not cause me to lose all social standing in elementary school. I assume she then drew circles on the top and on the sides where my head and arms would go and then removed the box and started cutting holes. Then she started drawing a replica of a gas pump with a big black magic marker. It was actually spot-on. It had regular and supreme and probably diesel. I think she put me in a black turtleneck and black pants and told me to keep my right arm bent, with my hand on my hip and my left arm straight out. Sort of like "I'm a little teapot / Short and stout / Here is my handle / Here is my spout." Except I wasn't a cute little teapot. I was a gas pump!!!!!! Here is my text conversation with my mom about this.

> **Me:** Hey mom, can you tell me exactly what was going through your mind when you made the decision that I would be a gas pump for Halloween in third grade?
>
> **Mom:** Probably had a box on hand that was the right size. Never liked store-bought costumes. Just a spur-of-the-moment idea that would be unique.
>
> **Me:** Haha! Remember I fell down the steps wearing that costume? I fell facedown in the stairwell! Stefi almost peed her pants!
>
> **Mom:** Did you spill any gas?

But everyone loved the costume. I got so much attention from the teachers, and I remember the high schoolers saying, "Check out the gas pump, that's so cool."

I believe I was priced at $1.00.

∞

When Avery was younger, he got in trouble at school for being mean to a girl. I told him that if he was mean to her one more time, I'd cut his hair and make him quit the baseball team. Avery loved his hair. And he loved the baseball team. I promised him that I'd do these things if I had one more call from the school about it.

I fully expected that he'd heed my warning.

When I got that second call that he was again being mean to that girl, my stomach fell. I had to follow through with my promise. It was awful. Avery was devastated when he realized that I meant business (even though I tried thinking of a way out of it).

I felt terrible calling the baseball coach, and I knew we let down the entire team. And the haircut, well, that was also horrible. Avery cried. I cried. Even the hairdresser cried.

The funny thing is, Avery moved on pretty quickly from this event that felt cataclysmic to me. I have not moved on so easily. I've thought about this story so many times. I've wondered if I did the right thing, if I went too far. Should I have changed the punishment to something lighter, or different, less impactful to others (like the entire baseball team)? It certainly made me think through what I'd said his punishment would be. But guess what? Avery never got into trouble again after that. No major trouble. Even though I look back and think maybe that was too harsh, I know that it worked. And from that point on, he believed every threat I ever made.

I do know my punishment for him was out of love and not out of anger. I loved him so much, and my girls, too, that I wanted to get it right with discipline. I know that with my oldest I had one shot at the first time he needed to know that I meant business. And I knew that if I threatened a punishment, I had to follow through or he would never believe me again.

Parenting throws you a lot to weigh, consider, and analyze. You need to make those apologies at times when you get it wrong. But one thing your children shouldn't doubt is your word. If you promise them something, see it through, but be careful what you promise, and I don't just mean in terms of discipline. In everything!

It's easy to promise your kids things in a moment because you just want them to leave you alone. You promise to do something fun tomorrow or to buy them something soon. Make sure you follow through.

One of the most important promises you can and should make to your children is that you'll be there for them always. Never, ever break that promise.

Make your word be worth something to your kids.

There is a lot of evil out there in the world. There always has been, but today it seems really dark. There are ideas being pushed on us that to me are from the pits of hell. One of the ways I have learned to de-stress when I feel like the world is going crazy, is to slow down a little and focus on my home and my family. And also pray. I'll go for a while and not check in with God, and I forget this. Then, before I know it, I feel like I'm on my own, and I'm overwhelmed with fear and stress. I have to remember to pray and get that peace that only God can provide, and read the Word. It's only then that I'm reminded that this is not our home and we have nothing to fear. There are some books that I love that help remind me of this, too. One is Frank Peretti's *This Present Darkness*, and the other is *The Screwtape Letters*, by C. S. Lewis. They both talk about the spiritual side of the world and how there are battles being fought over our souls and this world at all times. God always wins in the end. But it does really help me when I go back to the basics and slow down and remember the things that are truly important: loving God and loving others.

Chapter 15

#FAMILYISEVERYTHING

My grandparents were such a huge part of my life growing up. Sometimes it makes me sad that my kids don't have that. I was blessed to know all four of my grandparents very, very well and spent a lot of time with them. I think the family typically tends to spend more time with the maternal grandparents. I'm not sure why that is. I think that's something that women should ask themselves if they are being fair about. Because I've already told Avery that I'll kill him if he lets his wife do that. His kids will be as important to me as they are to his wife's parents, so women, do a little self-evaluation right now about that. And if you're not being fair and generous with your in-laws about the kids, change that, because what goes around comes around, and you might one day have a mean daughter-in-law.

Anyway, we spent a lot of time with all of our grandparents.

Grandma Evans worked in my school cafeteria in New Franklin, so I got to see her every day at lunch. And she always gave my friends and me extra food! Grandpa Evans was a farmer and was always tan. His skin looked like leather. He was always stepping outside to have a smoke. He was ornery, too. He used to try to drive my grandma crazy with the little things he did and said. When he sneezed, it was so loud it made the whole house shake, and she would say, "Albert! Well, for God's sake!" That was her stock answer for everything he did. To us the sneeze was hilarious, but I bet it infuriated her. Granny and Papa, my mom's parents, lived in Columbia, Missouri. This was about thirty minutes from New Franklin, so when we went there we tended to stay the night or the whole weekend. Granny had a true servant's heart. She doted on my grandpa. They both worked, but she was always the one to cook and clean and do the dishes and wash and fold and put away the clothes. She did all the Christmas shopping, grocery shopping, and, well, basically everything. Papa did the outside work, like mowing the yard and taking the trash to the curb and things like that, but the workload was by no means evenly distributed. Granny waited on everyone hand and foot, not just Papa. If you were in her house, you would for sure be fed and made to feel perfectly comfy and cozy. I am so much like her.

They also took us on summer vacations every year. We never went on a vacation with my parents, but Granny and Papa would take all the grandkids somewhere. They would do two different trips. One with the older grandkids—Jay, Matt, my cousins Scotty and Travis, and me. (I've always been the only girl. Most situations in my life have been me trying to keep up with older brothers, or me working in bands with all guys. That's why I understand men so well.) A lot of times we would just go to the Lake of the Ozarks in central Missouri, but we didn't care. It was all fun and ham sandwiches and chips and soda and laughter. I always got to sleep in the bed with Granny, and that was the best. She spoiled us rotten.

We still joke about this today, but every time we were in the car she would say, "Look, kids," and she would point out something on the road or in the town we were driving through. It would be nothing worth looking at, but she would always find something to point out and say, "Look, kids." Jay and his mother both have the "Look, kids" disease. They both love to look at buildings and restaurants and anything and everything when we are driving and they want you to love to look, too. The problem is, we are driving, so it goes by too fast to even see. I told Jay the Granny story years ago, and every time he shows us something he says, "Look, kids."

Another thing Granny and Papa did was take us out to dinner for our birthdays. These days people eat out all the freaking time and it's no big deal, but it was a big deal for us in the late seventies and in the eighties. We didn't get to be pampered in that way very often. Matt's birthday is March 2, and mine is February 5, so a lot of times we would do our birthday dinners together. I would give anything to be having dinner with Granny and Papa again. And I guess Matt can come, too. Do you see what an impact my Granny had on my life? I know God put my Granny into my life so I could feel that love, and so I would know how to take care of family and learn what it is to be a servant. This is what can and will happen when you really take the time to invest in your family. Especially children. Look at me, I'm forty-nine and still talking about my Granny.

My children have a different experience when it comes to grand-parents, because they have never lived in the same state as my parents. Many families are like that these days. Everyone is on the path they are supposed to be on, and I just have to believe that I have chosen the right one. There's no way I would have made it in music if I hadn't left

Missouri. My kids are close to my parents and love them very much. We just don't get to see them on a daily or weekly basis. I wish that was different, but we get home a good bit each year. We are there for nearly every graduation, every wedding, every big event. And I love going home.

The old saying is true, though: "Home is where the heart is." But it's also true that home is wherever your family is. We have spent so many years on the road and in and out of "normal life" that we know how to be at home wherever we are, as long as we are together. All my friends call me Hannah Montana because of how easily I slip into and out of being Sara Evans and Sara Barker. There have been many times when I would get off the bus just in time for a game's first pitch or kickoff. Somehow we make it all work. But you have to make family a priority.

To me, a cozy home is filled with the scent of food cooking or candles burning. It's couches with fluffy throws and pillows, and a kitchen always stocked with food and drinks. My tour bus is the same way. It's so warm and cozy and has all of our comforts of home.

When we used to have all seven kids together on Wednesday nights, I wanted them to relax, with the smell of home cooking wafting through the house. When their stomachs grew ravenous, I loved bringing them a plate, each dished up just for them. I remembered what each one liked and disliked, so the plates weren't served up the same. They were always so tired, too, on school nights. I would get them all blankets while they watched TV. To me, actions like these are the language of love. Words are important, but actions prove what we feel. This is true in every relationship we have. If you love someone, you show it—you don't just say it. One of my favorite John Mayer songs is called "Love Is a Verb." It's about that very thing. Love IS a verb. Love is action. You can't be a good mom, dad, friend, sister, brother, employee, or anything if you don't put effort into your relationships. You have to pursue those you love. You can't just tell someone you love them—you have to show them. And that's something I really try to do. I try to show the people in my life that I love them in many different ways, even if it's just a quick text when you have a spare minute to check up on someone. I know people who will go days and weeks without contacting their kids or grandkids or friends or parents. That shocks me. And if I am the only one doing the contacting, eventually I will assume that that person doesn't love me or want a relationship with me. I gravitate toward those who reciprocate my communication and pursue me, too.

Every time I post a pic of my immediate or extended family, I hashtag it #familyiseverything because I believe that family *is* everything. Strong families are the fabric of life. And good friends can also serve as family when you don't live where you grew up. I do get jealous sometimes when I see my girlfriends with their moms. Or knowing that their parents are staying with their kids while they are out of town. I would love to be able to see my mom anytime I wanted. Where is my private jet?

Chapter 16

TOO YOUNG TO BE OLD

I'm too young to be old and too old to be young.

—EVELYN COUCH,
IN THE MOVIE *FRIED GREEN TOMATOES*

I was shopping with my girls, who were fourteen and sixteen at the time. We were having a great time together, as we always do. I was feeling good about myself, having a day when everything was on point, or so I thought, until I stood next to them in the dressing room with that horrific lighting and saw us in the mirror. That was a rude awakening. First of all, why do they have horrific lighting in most dressing rooms? If I owned a clothing store, I'd light that dressing room to the point of false advertising, and I'd sell a lot more clothes because of it.

To be fair, the girls were teenagers. Teenagers tell their bodies to ignore whatever they just ate, and they listen. Their skin is flawless, their eyes have a constant sparkle, their bodies are tight, their hair is vibrant and luminous—all the things that we can't hold on to as hard as we try. There's no getting around it, youth is gorgeous. Getting older SUCKS.

When I saw myself in the mirror next to my girls, I didn't think I looked old or ugly or anything like that. I just didn't have that glow of youth like my daughters. It was a strange feeling, not competitive or jealous. It was one of those moments of impact when you face the reality that you aren't as young as you used to be. Or as young as your bitch daughters.

The thing is, I don't feel any different than when I was in my twenties or thirties. I feel like me. No age. Just me. Funny, fun, young, artistic, cool, hip, and happy. So it really hurt my feelings when my kids became teenagers and started saying, "Mom, you can't post that" or "Mom, stop dancing!" Like, really. Because it embarrassed me and made me feel OLD. So one time when one of them made a comment like that, I said, "Who the hell do you think you are to tell me that I can't post something or hashtag something, when you can't even pay for your own phone!" I might have said more than that, but that's not

Audrey, me, and Olivia

important. I get it, though—to them I'm just Mom. I always remind them and myself that J. Lo is older than I am.

I think women have it so much harder than men, too. Men look better with age a lot of times, but women are judged, mainly by each other. And I've never understood why people make jokes about how old someone is, or why people are embarrassed by how old they are. It's not our fault. Getting older as a female celebrity is even harder. In public, I am acutely aware of the constant stream of opinion about my weight, my hair, my age, my music, and so many other things. And I am my worst critic.

Sidenote: If you're a fan, and you come to a lot of shows, and you take pictures of me in action, please, please, please look at them before you post them. I have had so many otherwise happy days ruined after seeing an awful picture of me on stage. I'm serious. Because I move a lot and get so into my performance, some shots are just terrible. Especially if I'm not at my best weight. KK and Lesley and I dread looking at our phones some days because we fear what will be posted.

Isn't that sad that I even think that way? But we all do. Any of us who aren't naturally rail-thin.

When I entered my forties, I thought of one of my favorite movies, *Fried Green Tomatoes,* which is based on the book *Fried Green Tomatoes at the Whistle Stop Cafe,* by Fannie Flagg (the Whistle Stop Cafe is in Irondale, Alabama, just down the road from us). There's a scene in the movie when Kathy Bates's character, Evelyn Couch, says she feels lost because she is too young to be old and too old to be young.

Evelyn is not at the best stage of her life at this point in the movie. Her marriage is boring. Her husband pays more attention to the TV than to her. She's tired of trying to make herself better through self-help classes and books. She's middle-aged and doesn't know who she is anymore. Then she meets Ninny Threadgoode.

Ninny is an old woman in a nursing home. Evelyn finds solace listening to her stories. Ninny has lived a long life and has had rich life experiences. One day while talking, Evelyn expresses her fear of getting old and dying, and Ninny says, "I wouldn't be afraid of death if I was you. I'd be more afraid of drivin' in rush hour traffic."

Evelyn realizes that Ninny isn't afraid of death because her life has been so full and meaningful. At some point, I think every woman feels a little like Evelyn, and we long to be like Ninny—at peace with our age and confident about the future beyond this life.

I've heard that a woman hits a point where she accepts her age, what she looks like, and who she is. I've met women like that, like Ninny Threadgoode in *Fried Green Tomatoes*. They are women who just live without fear. My mother is like that, and so were my grand-mothers. I hope to be that way, too, but the truth is, I'm not there yet. I hope there is that magical time when I find contentment with my age. But right now, getting older is not easy. I still have a lot of dreams and goals and new things I'm pursuing. My children are growing up quickly and soon will start leaving the nest. Life is changing, but it's always changing. And that just has to be okay.

If I'm going to feel good about the way I look, I have to be in good shape. I have a "sweet spot" in my weight that I love, and if I go over that at all, I don't love it. Being unhappy with how you look is hard enough, but being unhappy with how you look in front of millions of people is another thing. I know exactly what to do and how to do it to keep myself in shape, but why do I undo my hard work sometimes? It drives me crazy. The best way for me to diet is just not to eat as much as I think I want or can. Or whenever I want to. I believe strongly in the "eat when you're hungry, stop when you're full" method.

My sister Lesley introduced me to the Weigh Down diet. The basic premise is that you shouldn't eat until and unless you are truly hungry. Like, you know, when you haven't eaten for four or five hours and your stomach starts to growl. And you are . . . wait for it . . . HUNGRY!!!!!!!!! That is when you should eat. And you should eat whatever you want. But the catch is, you HAVE to stop when you are satisfied. Not stuffed or even full, satisfied. I believe this is how God intended for us to eat. It's how kids eat. When a kid is hungry he will eat, and when he's full, he will stop eating and go play again. That's what we as adults need to do. Stop eating when we are satisfied and go play. Every single time I have done this, I have lost weight. Every single time. But it takes discipline. It sounds simple, but it's not easy.

The program called the Weigh Down is actually a church based in Nashville. The lady who started it preaches that it's a sin to eat when you're not hungry. The sin of gluttony. I see what she is saying, but like all things that start out in the name of God and are then used to scare and control people, this turned me off. I couldn't get into buying the books and going to the meetings, and I refused to feel guilty if ever I did overeat. I know that my salvation does not involve my mistakes. Jesus died on the cross to cover all of my sins and yours. I believe that. Therefore I am saved whether I commit the sin of gluttony or not.

We gain weight if we eat when we are not hungry. And usually if we eat when we aren't hungry, we will overeat. I also don't think it's a good idea to restrict certain foods. Everyone I know who restricts certain foods will lose at first but then gain it all back, and then some. Eventually you are going to put those foods back into your life, and when you do, you will eat too much of them. I tried a no-carb diet once, and I ate the toppings of three pizzas one night because 1) I thought I was going to have a panic attack at the thought of never eating pizza crust again, and 2) I thought, well, they said I could eat anything besides carbs, so I overate on the other things. And I was so stuffed! No one should eat even one whole pizza topping, much less three.

Anytime I let someone else come in and tell me how to be skinny, it doesn't work. Because I know what works for my body, and that is to not eat unless my stomach is growling, and to stop when I'm satisfied. And as far as exercise goes, I NEVER lose weight with exercise or working out, unless I eat the Weigh Down way. I love to play any sport, especially tennis, and I love to walk fast and be active. Every time I hire a trainer, they just come over and work me to the point of killing me and it makes me so fat. And I'm always so sore that I can't function.

It's funny how people are so stubborn about the simple solutions. They want to believe that it can't be that easy. It's like Christianity. The Bible says, in John 3:16, "For God so loved the world that He gave His only begotten Son, that whosoever believes in Him shall not perish, but have everlasting life." Boom. Simple. All you have to do is believe that Jesus Christ was sacrificed on the cross to forgive us our sins, past, present, and future. And we will be with Him forever in Heaven.

The sad thing is, people are convinced—by those who want to control us and make money off us—that things aren't that simple. If someone comes in and promises you that you'll lose weight if you eat this, or drink this, or take this pill, you are inclined to believe it. You buy what they are selling. We are brainwashed into thinking we have to follow all these rules. It starts in preschool. "Stand in a straight line, everyone walk the same way, raise your hand before you can talk, everyone learn at the same pace, we are all the same, same, same, same, and do not try to color outside of the lines."

We are not all the same, and we do not all have to think the same way. One way that we are the same is that we are all children of God, and He loves us and only wants our hearts. So believe in yourself, and trust YOUR OWN GUT, and do what you believe is right for you and your family. When it comes to weight loss, you know when you're eating too much and too often. Let your body tell you when it needs food—not your brain, your body. Your brain will lie to you. Your brain will say, "I'm bored, I should eat something. I'm depressed, I should eat. I'm celebrating, I should eat!" But your stomach, if you really listen, will say, "You just had food two hours ago and you are not hungry right now. I'll growl when it's time to eat again."

One thing that can really help keep me looking great and feeling young is the right clothes. I hate it when I make fashion mistakes, especially on stage. Because like I said, a bad picture that gets posted makes for a very bad day. I have a certain look that I like when I'm on stage that makes me feel right. And anytime I veer away from that, I am mad at myself when I see pics of it.

I like to wear things that make me feel tough and sexy at the same time. My favorite look on stage is flared jeans and a great button-down shirt tucked in. Actually, the jeans don't always have to be flared, they just have to look great. I wore one of my favorite outfits ever when I performed on the Lionel Richie tribute TV show—and I always say this was one of the best performances of my career. I sang "Endless Love" with Marc Anthony and it was amazing! Truly amazing. We had never met until the day before, when we had dress rehearsals. It was in Vegas the day after the Academy of Country Music (ACM) Awards in 2012. I was at my very best as far as my weight, hair, skin, everything goes. KK and I always have fittings before big events like these, and it makes her job so much easier if I am skinny! Because everything looks good and there are so many more options. So she brought these Rag & Bone jeans that were black in the front and white in the back. They were skinny jeans, and we paired them with these amazing nude pumps that had black six-inch heels. We put a simple black long-sleeve button-down shirt with them. We left it unbuttoned really far down and put a sexy black lace tank under it. Then she put this huge necklace with it. It was blue and black, just perfect for the outfit. KK is so great at accessories. My hair was super-long and she waved it—I like my hair either straight or wavy, NOT curly. Everything was on point. And the song sounded so perfect. Lionel Richie was freaking out in the audience, and we got a standing ovation. I highly recommend that you watch this on YouTube.

Another time I felt like I was the epitome of what I expect myself to look like was at the CMT Crossroads performance that I did with Joe Walsh from the Eagles. Again, I was exactly where I like to be weight-wise, making the wardrobe selection so much easier. I wore these snakeskin skinny jeans and a tan shirt that was just kind of flowy and had billowy sleeves, and sexy pumps. I don't know what KK had for breakfast that day, but she did my makeup just about as well as she's ever done! She put a deep blue eye shadow right in the crease and the perfect color of blush and lip gloss. I absolutely loved it. We sang "Best of My Love" together, and that was one of the biggest honors of my career, to sing with Joe Walsh.

Another great red carpet moment was the 2011 CMA Awards. KK got me a stunning one-shoulder maroon gown by designer David Meister, and a gorgeous navy-blue necklace by Hyla DeWitt that was big and chunky and hung close to my collarbone. I wore my hair very plain. I washed it and KK blew it dry and we left it like that. The gown was slinky-tight, almost like spandex or something, and it went to the floor, with a slight train following it. It was my favorite gown that I've ever worn. It perfectly matched my personality. I actually hate dresses and gowns. They are almost all hideous on me because they usually don't hug the right parts, and they show the wrong parts. I like to show my legs a lot and not my arms. I love short dresses with long sleeves.

I used to love that show *What Not to Wear*. There are some people who really just don't know what to wear and what not to wear. On the show, they would start by secretly videotaping whoever had been selected as the subject of the episode. Then they sit down with her and demonstrate to her why her fashion choices are not working. They go to her house and take all her clothes and bring them to the TV studio. They make her try on some of her favorite outfits and look at herself in a three-way mirror. That usually does the trick, because almost no one has a three-way mirror in her house. When the person begins to relent, they just chuck everything into the trash and help her shop for a new wardrobe. Then she gets a hair and makeup make-over. By the end of the show, she is happy and looks amazing, and in her post-show interview a few weeks later, she talks about how her life has changed for the better since she learned what not to wear. I know there are much bigger things in the world to worry about, but it is true that looking great and wearing the right kind of clothes for your body type can really boost your mood.

The small things are just as important to me as the big ones. White teeth, great eyebrows, great skin, and a spray tan. These things all add to my overall style. Cute toes and fingernails. Details matter.

I don't like to wear sneakers unless I'm walking or working out or playing tennis. I don't know why, but I don't think I look cute in them. I always take flip-flops with me when I play tennis, and as soon as I am done playing, I take the tennis shoes off and put the flip-flops on. A lot of times I will play tennis in the morning and then meet a friend for lunch, and I'm fine to wear the tennis skirt and a cute jacket, but if I keep the tennis shoes on I feel like a total dork. But I feel cute in the flip-flops.

I would always rather wear a pair of low-waisted bell-bottom jeans that make my butt look great than a pair of leggings. I'm talking about comfort. Same with shorts. I always prefer cutoff denim shorts, especially if they are soft material and low-waisted, over a cute pair of workout shorts. Every time I try to do that look with tennis shoes and the cute Lululemon tops, I just cry and go back to bed. That look is not in line with my personality. Even though I'm a great athlete. I'd just rather kick your butt in jeans.

I also hate t-shirts. I mean, I love cute, stylish t-shirts, but I hate normal t-shirts. Like the ones that have been made for a school or a fundraiser. Those look horrible on me.

Also, I freak out when I see any gray hairs. That is something that just drives me crazy, and I run to my colorist right away. As much as I hate harsh overhead lighting, sometimes it's helpful because I can see every gray that might be popping through. I know that coloring your hair can be expensive and time-consuming, and it's hard to get an appointment sometimes, but I think there's a line you have to draw where you won't allow your roots to grow out too long. You can always get a root touch-up kit to do at home. I've never understood women who walk around with an inch of gray growing on either side of their middle part and the rest of their hair is colored. Maybe I care more than I should; I just don't want to have gray hair yet.

For me, it's about what makes me feel confident and what makes me feel insecure. And I think confidence is attractive in both men and women. I have a little more pep in my step when I feel good about the way I look.

I never want to stop trying and being my best. I have a perfectionist mentality. I'm not a quitter. I never have been. I'm really competitive, so I like to see how much I can push myself to try to be the best me every single day.

Chapter 17

DIVORCE

Let me just tell you how much I hate divorce. Even though I've been through one, I still maintain that it's one of the worst things a human being can go through. Especially if you have kids, or you're the kid whose parents are splitting up. In divorce, people do and say things that they never thought themselves capable of. Divorce is one of the most destructive things that can happen to a family. And the kids are almost always the ones who get torn in two.

I think you should at least try a lot of counseling before making the decision to divorce. If it seems inevitable and nothing is working, then you need to sit together with a pastor or a counselor and possibly some relatives or close friends and come up with a plan for how you are going to tell the children and what you are going to tell them. You need to have a solid list of things that you can tell them that won't leave them scared and lost. Like:

1. Mommy and Daddy love you guys more than anything in the world and that will never change.
2. This is NOT your fault.
3. You will ALWAYS see both of us ANYTIME you want.
4. We are BOTH still your parents and always will be.
5. We will BOTH continue to be at all of your events.
6. We will BOTH support you and take care of you.
7. We will BOTH work together to parent you just like before.
8. You can ask us anything and we will be honest with you.
9. You are safe.
10. We promise not to fight over you or talk about money, child support, alimony, bills, cars, sports gear, etc., in front of you.
11. We will do our best to remain civil and even friends for your sake.
12. We will not talk badly about the other parent in front of you.
13. If either of us remarries, we won't let the stepparent take the place of your parent.
14. We will always be your parents forever and always love you.

These are just a few of the many things you need to reassure your kids about. If you are going through a divorce and your parents did not divorce, you have no idea what the children are going through. It is pain and stress and anxiety that will take them a very long time to get past, but it will take a hell of a lot longer if you misbehave during and after divorce. Moms, you should never tell your kids to ask their dads for the child support check. You should never involve them in any of those issues. It's child abuse. Plain and simple. Moms and Dads, never talk badly about the other parent or the other parent's new spouse, if there is one. Children have enough to deal with without you making them stressed and basically telling them not to love their new step-mom or stepdad. That, too, is child abuse.

When you already have kids and then stepkids come into the family, you have to be sensitive to your own kids and never let them think that you're trying too hard to please your stepkids. Same goes for the father who isn't living with his kids anymore but is now living with his stepkids. He has to be careful to explain to his children that he doesn't love the stepkids more just because he sees them more. And if you're a divorced dad and your ex has remarried, you are also dealing with the pain of another man living with your kids. It's probably the most complex and difficult situation a family can go through. But if you have God in your family, and you have love in your heart and no bitterness or unforgiveness for your ex, it can be done well with as little pain as possible. Unfortunately, the adults are almost always the ones who mess everything up. I haven't been perfect and have definitely made mistakes and said and done things I wish I hadn't. But I know my intentions have always been good and I've acted out of love.

∞

I think divorce is really tough on dads. He feels guilty. He feels guilty about the divorce, even if it wasn't his fault. He feels like he is at a huge disadvantage (and he usually is) when it comes to the kids taking the "mom's side" on everything because they usually end up primarily living with her. Even if she caused the divorce and left the marriage, they can still live with her. So he goes from raising his kids on a daily basis and taking them to school and picking them up from school and putting them to bed to NOTHING. They can become almost like strangers. Especially if the mom is insecure and determined to turn her kids against him. And here's the thing, even if your ex did something awful, or cheated, I still believe that you shouldn't talk badly about him to your kids, unless he is a danger to them emotionally, spiritually, or physically. Then you can tell your kids some things that they might need to know to help them.

If you're a divorced dad, you still need to put your own comfort and feelings aside and discipline your kids the way they deserve to be disciplined. Discipline them as though you were raising them on a daily basis. Even though you want them to love you and you know you're most likely being talked about, it's still the right thing for the child. As their father, you have to take an active role in their lives, even if the mother won't let you. And vice versa if you're a divorced mom not living with your kids. You are still their parent and you have to fight for the right to be their parent. You have to ask for things like schedules and doctors' appointments and anything they are involved in. And if you are a divorced parent who is trying to keep those things from the other parent, you are so wrong. Stop making life an internal hell for your kids. I know kids who are literally afraid to speak to their dads when they are at an event with their mom, and vice versa. I mean, in what world is that okay to do to a child? You may have divorced your spouse, but your children didn't divorce their parent, so don't act like that. You need to encourage the relationship between your ex and your kids.

Of course, if your ex is causing emotional or physical harm to your children, then you need to take steps to stop him from being able to be around your kids, or at least make it supervised. And definitely if you have left a marriage because you were being abused, then that needs to be addressed in the divorce. It may be possible for the kids to only see the abuser in a supervised setting.

Chapter 18

FINDING THE PERFECT BLEND

Blending a family is not for the faint of heart, and it's not for the unkind heart. Incredible challenges lie ahead when you decide to marry someone with kids. Our Barker blended family isn't perfect, but like everything else in my life, I try to make it as perfect as an imperfect situation can be. Blended families can be a huge blessing. Maybe when all is said and done, a blended family might become the greatest blessing a family can have. Children can have more people to love them, more people to call on and support them when they need it. They may get experiences and insights they wouldn't have had otherwise.

But to have any chance of a blended family becoming a blessing, you have to *make it happen*. You can't just hope it'll work out well. You can't wish it or pray for it. You have to pray for it AND work on it—all the time. Most important, you have to remember that the only person's behavior you can control is your own. And if you're a step-parent, don't be any of the following:

- The overbearing or dominant person who believes she should have too much say in raising her stepkids
- The jealous kind who acts as if he is competing with his stepkids for his spouse's time
- The absentee individual who is completely hands-off and often behaves as if stepkids are guests to be temporarily tolerated
- The person who is overly critical because she sees her spouse's ex in the stepkids

Keep in mind: Kids are the innocent victims of divorce. So just love them. Seriously. You can't be a great stepparent if you're a jealous, selfish, petty person.

If you're a stepparent, envision yourself in a role similar to that of a mentor, an older sibling, or an aunt or uncle. These aren't unimportant roles; these individuals can be key, life-changing people in a young person's life. Tell your stepchildren that this is the role you see yourself in, and that you aren't trying to replace a mom or a dad.

I always wanted Jay's kids and my kids to know the clear message. We love you ALL. No one needs to feel jealous or insecure because we're here for you 1,000 percent. Like when Braxton and Avery played against each other in football, we made t-shirts for Olivia and Audrey that were half Avery's school and half Braxton's. Jay and I clapped for both teams.

I said it already, but this needs to be said more than once. This is a big one with me. Don't discipline your stepkids! That's it. There's no quicker way to create hatred in a stepchild. The evil stepmother stereotype was created for a reason. I've seen stepdads acting almost like bullies in the house, demanding respect and for rules to be followed. No one respects someone like that. Instead of being a role model, that stepfather won't be able to influence his stepchildren in any good or profound way. He's just a bully. The only time you should ever discipline stepchildren is if you are left in charge of them and they are young. Obviously you have to look after them, and that might entail some correcting, but even a babysitter has to do that. Also, if you become the stepparent and the other mom or dad isn't in the picture, then you can discipline a bit more. But be cautious, and err on the side of just letting your spouse do most of it. You can be there for support. Of course, you may discipline a stepchild if he is causing harm to the family and/or the other kids in the home. Then you have every right to speak to him directly and correct him. But be fair.

Talk to your stepchildren about their feelings and your feelings. Try not to let your feelings keep you from really hearing what they're saying, but don't engage like a friend. Remember, you are the adult, so maintain that respectable role of an aunt or mentor. Be sure that however you talk to your stepchildren, you'd be perfectly fine talking and acting the same way in front of either of their parents.

Expect them to test you, your love for them, and your spouse's love for them. Don't be angry when this happens, because it's inevitable. If you think you have a perfect blended family, think again—they will test you off and on, and often for reasons you'll never understand. As kids grow and go through different stages, they'll have ups and downs with how they feel about the blended situation and how they process the loss of their original family unit (even if that was years earlier, they're always going to wonder what might have been). They'll go through insecurities and fears, anger and confusion and jealousy, that will be associated with growing up and becoming adults. So expect it.

Continue to provide that unwavering, loving, secure home where they can find acceptance and love. They'll get through it, and so will you.

Basically, make your stepkids' second home a wonderful place. Create the kind of home they want to come to. Make it a haven from the outside world, and a safe place where they can spend time with the parent they don't get to be with all the time. If you're married to a divorced dad, do everything you can to foster his relationship with his kids. Sometimes that means just staying out of the way. There are a lot of Wednesday nights when I tell Jay to go to dinner with his kids without us. I think they need that alone time with their dad every now and then.

This is important! Remember, your stepkids are being raised differently in their other home, and you have to be aware of that and be okay with it. They may be getting different messages in their other house. There is nothing you can do about that. Show compassion and support, and remember that consistent message of unconditional love and acceptance.

Don't compete with your stepchildren's other home. Blending a family is NOT a competition with the other parent. Create your own home and family experiences that don't conflict or compete with the other. Remember that you are all raising these precious humans in less than perfect conditions. Make it as perfect as imperfect can be, and just be a good person.

Serve them. Do special little things that will show you care. Don't expect much in return, especially in the current moment. Remember that stepparenting is oftentimes a thankless job, and sometimes it takes decades for kids to realize that a stepparent was really good to them when they were growing up. Give out of true love for them and for your spouse. Whether it looks like it or not, those kids are dealing with a broken family day in and day out. If you can offer small comforts and security, you are helping to mend their brokenness, even if the results aren't immediately visible.

Do some activities that the entire family can enjoy. Sports has always been a real connecting point between my kids and Jay's. Everybody in our family loves to play sports, and I think Jay's kids were really happy and excited when they realized how athletic I am and how much I LOVE to play anything. Games, competitions, swimming, basketball, softball, soccer, Ultimate Frisbee, football, cards, board games—you name it, and I'll play it. Up until about four to five years ago, I could even beat them all in a footrace, which they actually loved. With a dad who has been so successful at sports and in his career, Jay's kids put a high value on success in those areas, and they appreciate that I'm also successful in those ways.

Sometimes a stepkid will resist participating in a family activity and will want to make everyone else miserable, too (they are testing you or just aren't happy!). Maybe that child doesn't feel heard or understood and is showing that to you. Try to figure out what the issue is and deal with it head-on. Be sure you get things out on the table so there's never a buildup of resentment. It may not be easy to figure out. Try to work together, express the fact that you care, and try to find compromises—but the entire family can't be made to suffer for that holdout.

It's a process, and you have to be patient with each other.

While feeling love for stepchildren may not be natural like it was with your own children, look for things to love about your stepkids, and actively love them even if the natural feeling isn't there. Love will grow. Care about your stepkids' hearts, interests, and struggles.

Someday, when all of the kids in our house are grown, I want each of them to remember our consistent message. They are all loved. We will always be there for them. We are a family.

Chapter 19

SUNDAY DINNERS

The weekend is nearly over, and we're in that cusp between the end of one week and the start of the next. I'm making Sunday dinner. Cooking for this family of nine isn't a chore. It's actually one of my favorite things to do.

Sunday dinner brings my own childhood rolling back to me. Growing up, we worked hard all week. Yet no matter the workday or season, my mom served us great meals three times a day. But my favorite meal of the week was Sunday dinner.

We'd go to church on Sunday morning, and the rest of the day was lighter on chores than other days. Then we'd head to Granny and Papa's house, and usually all my uncles, aunts, and cousins joined up for the feast.

Granny and Papa Floyd had a huge finished basement in their house. All the kids would race down there, and we'd just go wild.

Sometimes we'd make up games. Or we'd play with a bowling set or it would be hide-and-seek. We were loud and rambunctious, and nothing could be more fun for a child. At some point, we'd get the call to come eat. Sufficiently worn-out and with stomachs growling, we'd head upstairs and get welcomed by the smell of Granny's delicious comfort food.

Sunday dinners went through a rough patch during that difficult season when Mom and Dad got divorced. Later, when my grandparents grew older, the tradition moved to our farmhouse, with my mom cooking for the family. Anyone could show up for Sunday dinner, and there was always enough food. The house simmered with the smell of good ole country cooking: brisket, turkey, fried chicken, baked chicken, homemade chicken and dumplings, peach pie, pecan pie, Missouri dirt cake.

Even today, if I were to show up on a Sunday afternoon at Mom's house in Missouri, she'd be setting out food and there'd be enough for everyone.

As much as I love to work and be in the studio, or writing, or on stage, I also love the days when I am home with my family and there is a fire going in the fireplace and I'm cooking a huge meal for everyone. I absolutely love to sit down at our big wooden dining room table with a glass of wine and enjoy a big dinner. I adore watching people I love eat food that I've prepared for them. My three kids are huge talkers. They love to sit with me for hours and talk and talk and talk about everything under the sun. They are deep thinkers, too, and love to exhaust any topic. This they get from my side of the family for sure. If you ever were to be at Sunday dinner at Mom's (she is Granny Pat now), you can be sure that hours will go by, after the meal has been devoured, with us just talking and laughing and telling and retelling stories. It's one of my favorite things to do in life.

During the week, I cook most every night, or else we get takeout to eat at home. We'll sit in the living room and watch TV together. I enjoy dishing up the plates and bringing the food to each person. We eat and laugh together as we watch our favorite shows. I want school nights to be comfortable and relaxing, with no pressure at all. The Barker house is a haven for each family member. We have food, our Apple TV, swimming in the backyard, basketball, music that we share, and Ping-Pong, and we go through our board game phases. Cozy, cozy, cozy is the goal. That and smiles all around.

And then on Sundays we sit around the dining room table. I love the tradition of Sunday dinner and am passing that on to my children. I make our favorite recipes on this day, and we don't worry about calories or carbs, or really anything, for that matter. We just gather together, we talk and laugh, we share stories and jokes, and we fill our bellies.

I'm Midwest-born, but I'm southern at heart. I love everything having to do with good manners, respect, and being polite. One of my big pet peeves is when someone gets their meal and they don't grab a napkin to go with it. I mean, this actually blows my mind because I cannot conceive of eating without a napkin. Am I the only one who feels this way? I have been preaching this to all of our kids for ten years, and yet some of them STILL do not get a napkin. I see them take a bite of chicken fingers dipped in honey mustard and then wipe their hands on their pants or t-shirt! I go cray-cray. Because they aren't the one who has to wash those clothes and spray Shout on them to get the honey mustard, grease, and ketchup stains out!

I also hate paper plates. I secretly judge women who serve meals on paper plates. Especially dinner. To me that feels like giving up, like wearing sweats every day. There are just some things that we shouldn't let go of. Honestly, in this day and age, it feels like we have given up on a lot of things that really matter. It's hard to hold the full attention of anyone just for one full sentence before they look at their phone. It makes me sad. I think we should never stop making an effort to hold on to the simple and precious things in life.

Chapter 20

THE GOOD OLD DAYS

One of my favorite shows of all time is *The Dick Van Dyke Show*. First of all, it's absolutely hilarious. The producer and writer, Carl Reiner, was a comedic genius, and Dick Van Dyke brilliantly delivers every line. I absolutely love Mary Tyler Moore as well. For years, every time I stayed in a hotel, I put my room under the name Laura Petrie, Mary Tyler Moore's character's name. Every day she gets up early, dresses impeccably, and gets breakfast ready for her husband, Rob Petrie, and their son, Ritchie. Rob commutes into New York City, and when he comes home every evening around 6:00 p.m., Laura has dinner ready with the table set. They have coffee and dessert after every meal. They are so polite and civilized. Their house is so cozy, too. It all seems perfect, and I know it's not reality, but again . . . why not strive for perfection?

I recently downloaded all the *Dick Van Dyke Show* episodes and have been showing them to Jay and the kids. They love it and we laugh so hard. Here's the other thing I love about it. It's funny—no, it's hilarious—without being crude. I'm not a prude, but I think it's easy to make crude sexual jokes, and I don't find them to be funny. They make me uncomfortable. Hollywood definitely goes too far, especially in how they try to sexualize our youth way too soon. When you watch shows like *Dick Van Dyke* or *Carol Burnett* or *Andy Griffith*, you realize what true talent and brilliance really is. Anyone can say something perverted or crass or downright evil to try to be funny, but it takes real talent to make people laugh with smart writing and awesome physical comedy.

I think a lot of people probably feel the same way I do about the world. I know I'm only in my forties, but I miss "the good ole days" when people sat in a room and talked to each other, or looked at the world going by while riding in a car—the beauty of nature, the awesomeness of big cities. I feel like everyone is missing everything in order to look at nothing on a phone. I'm guilty of it, too. It's impossible not to be. Even as I write this book, I stop every ten minutes or so and check my phone. I'm addicted. I have to make sure I'm not missing any texts or emails, and I'm always connected.

The phone is one of my biggest pet peeves in life. Jay and I hardly ever fight, but that is definitely something we do fight about, THE PHONE. Like if we are going to sit down and watch a show together, I don't think he should get on Twitter. There's no way you can hear the dialogue and really be watching a show if you're looking at your phone! It's so hard not to nag him about that, and Jay does not like to be nagged. But I told him years ago that I needed "permission" to nag about two things: 1) him being on his phone all the time and 2) when he tailgates. These two things infuriate me.

If I am on my phone and someone starts to talk to me, I always try to immediately look up at them to listen. Or if I am listening to someone talk, I try never to go to my phone. I always try to wait until they are done, or I say, "Excuse me one second, I'm not trying to be rude, but I need to check to see if so-and-so texted me." I have seen people flat-out ignore everyone in the room and just look at Facebook or Instagram for an entire evening. People, please, please stop doing this. It's ruining our lives and our relationships and making us very, very stupid. Not to mention how unbelievably rude it is. Parents, don't just accept this behavior from your kids. Don't shrug your shoulders and say, "My kid is always on his phone and there's nothing I can do about it—it's just how kids are these days." NO! When you see them ignoring you or anyone because they are looking at their phones or taking selfies, call them out on it. Call them out on it in front of other people so it embarrasses them. I have no problem disciplining my kids to a certain degree in front of other people.

This phone obsession is a sign of the times and shows the disintegration of our society. I wish there was more value put on human life. Everyone has the same right to have a chance at life. The unborn, victims of human trafficking, people who are addicted to drugs. It's like we've become hardened and calloused to the sanctity and preciousness of the lives of others, so that we can have whatever we want. I wish we could all love each other above ourselves, the way Jesus taught us to. That's really all He spoke about was loving others, being selfless, and loving God with all our hearts. I think if everyone would think about love first, the world would be a much better and safer place to live. Laura and Rob remind me so much of Granny and Papa. They lived very much like that. With simplicity, honor, goodness, respect, good manners, dignity, and love.

Growing up in a big family, or at least in my big family, you had to learn the art of conversation and humor. If I had to name just one thing I am most thankful for that I got from my mother, I would hands down say her sense of humor. She raised us with comedy and wit and brilliance of conversation. She is the best storyteller, and I got that from her. And she is a genius at comedy and comedic timing. I feel sorry for people who weren't raised with funny parents. I have always been so crazy and funny and quick-witted with my kids, and now they are hilarious, too. Not everyone is born with a sense of humor, but you can definitely teach people—your spouse, your friends—to be funny. All of my kids' friends know that 90 percent of what I am going to say to them is going to be sarcastic or funny. I believe laughter and good conversation is the cure for most everything. I have very strict rules for my family about good conversation. For instance, no one can have their phones out during a dinner. Actually, I'll explain it this way—here are the times when phones are prohibited:

1. At dinner
2. During family conversation
3. Anytime someone is talking
4. When the family is watching something on TV together
5. When I'm talking to my kids
6. When we are listening to a song (There are many rules for this one. You really aren't allowed to talk at all, and should barely even breathe, if someone is playing a song. Is that too much? I don't think so.)
7. After I realize you've been on your phone too long
8. When someone is trying to show everyone something on TV
9. When someone is telling a story (more about this in a minute)

Conversation is definitely a LOST art. We have another strict rule in our family: NO SIDE-TALKING. You know those people who turn to the person next to them and start side-talking while someone is telling a story? What is that? I want you to ask yourself right now if you do that. If you do, never do it again. Or if you're that person who starts talking to a dog while someone is trying to tell a story, STOP!!!!!!!!!! Don't you know how rude this is? It brings the conversation to a halt.

Some people are oblivious to how they are. Parents, don't let your kids be oblivious to how they are, and also, don't let them do things that annoy you. I may be wrong, but I believe that a lot of kids will try to do and say things that are dorky or nerdy, and as parents it's our job to say, "Hey, baby, don't do that. It's really not funny and makes you seem weird." Why is it bad for a parent to do that in a gentle and loving way?

You're teaching your child how to interact properly with people. I remember when Audrey was a toddler, she had the tendency to be OCD. She wanted everything in her world to be a certain way. She was so particular about how her socks felt, or how her jacket felt around her arms, or if her gloves weren't on just right. And I had to put a stop to it. I didn't want her to grow up thinking it was okay to be that freaked out by little things not being exactly the way she wanted them. I see other parents who totally indulge their kids in whatever they want all the time, and they are creating little monsters and adults who are odd and annoying and can't cope with life. If a mom says, "She has to have it exactly this way or she throws a fit," I always think to myself, "Let her throw the fit now and teach her to be more flexible." After all, shouldn't we as the parents make the rules and set the boundaries?

We have gotten so out of control in our society about some things.

We are afraid to parent. We are afraid to hurt our kids' feelings by telling them no, or being honest with them about how they are coming across. That's not parenting—it's babysitting. The babysitter doesn't care about the child's long-term well-being; she just wants to get through the night and keep the kid alive until the parents get home and pay her. But true love is talking to your kids honestly about everything and telling them no. One of my favorite comedians is Tim Hawkins, and he does a hilarious bit about giving your kids the gift of "no." Truly, that is actually a gift. And believe me, parents, I have not been perfect about this. It's hard. It's really, really hard to tell your kids no. These are little people whom we love more than anything or anyone in this world, so to punish them or tell them no is so opposed to our instincts. But even God, who loves us perfectly, tells us no at times. Remember the Garth Brooks song "Unanswered Prayers"? "Sometimes I thank God / For unanswered prayers . . ."

We cannot ignore what we know is the best thing for our kids because it makes us feel better. To me, that is one of the most selfish and self-centered things a parent can do—not discipline your child because it makes you feel better.

Chapter 21

LOOKING FORWARD

As life always shows us, nothing can forever stay the same, and everything evolves and changes, even if we desperately want it to stay the way it is. One example is an amazingly weird change that just happened. My mom and stepfather MOVED off the farm! The farm that I had grown up on since I was fourteen! It was a cute old white farmhouse that only had two bathrooms.

My mom and stepfather are reaching a point in their lives where they do not need all that land—nor can they care for it and I understand them downsizing. They moved closer to New Franklin, into a beautiful cottage-style house on a beautiful property right on the outskirts of our quaint little town. It's been very stressful for my mom. Moving is stressful anyway. I can't imagine doing it after living somewhere for more than thirty years!

Jay and I decided last year that we wanted to be adventurous and find a sixties ranch-style home in Mountain Brook and gut it and remodel it. Worst decision of my life. Well, not the worst, but probably in the top ten. We found an awesome 4,500-square-foot ranch up on a hill on three acres with the backyard overlooking downtown Birmingham. It's absolutely gorgeous. We had just spent a few weeks in Malibu, and we thought, let's make this a Hollywood Hills home—this feels like Malibu! We were off and running.

We hired a general contractor and, of course, my friend Lisa as the decorator. The house actually turned out beautiful, and we love it, but I don't think I would ever want to completely remodel again. It really brought out the absolute worst in me. I like to think of myself as a very kind and patient person who tries to see and believe the best in people. I expect people to do business the way I do business, and it's just not that way in the construction world.

Our house wasn't ready on move-in day. It had not been cleaned, so there was a three-inch-thick layer of dust over the entire house when Lisa and her mom (her business partner) showed up to meet the moving company. Lisa called me frantically, telling me not to come over because she knew I would have a meltdown. So she and her mom and our house manager, Lavilla, scrubbed that house while the movers waited patiently until it was move-in ready. I will never be able to thank them enough for that. When she called us to come over, the house was already looking great. But that's just one of those things that the contractor should have taken care of, and it would have saved us all a ton of stress.

Even after we moved in, there was still so much work to be done. For almost three months, we were waking up with someone in our house working at all times (when we could get them there). I'm sure everyone reading this book who has ever built or remodeled a home is saying, "Hell yes, girl! Preach it! We've been there, done that!"

Working with that contractor was honestly one of the worst experiences of my life. It was way over budget and way behind schedule, and much of the work was shoddy. We had to hire different people to fix what he didn't do right.

The decorating was truly beautiful, but that's because of what Lisa and I picked out. It's very Hollywood Hills, very glamorous, with lots of black walls and crazy wallpaper and black hardwood floors. I've only lived in a ranch home one other time in my life, right after Avery was about three months old, and I lived in it until after my daughter Olivia was born. I really like them because everyone feels closer. I love hearing the kids on the phone or their music playing or their conversations with their friends, as opposed to being so far away from them upstairs.

After the horrible experience of remodeling, we started considering a move back to Nashville. Both of my girls wanted to try online school so that they could travel with me all the time and start pursuing their own careers in entertainment. We found an amazing house in Nashville, so we put the ranch house on the market and it sold quickly. Now we are back in Nashville!

∞

After Avery graduated from high school in 2018, he moved to Nashville. He decided, and I wholeheartedly agreed, that college WAS NOT for him. Avery is so smart and got very high scores on his ACT, but he hated school. He is a natural-born musician. He felt like college would be a waste of time and money, when he could just dive head-first into music. I was so worried to tell my friends that Avery wasn't going to go to college, because in Mountain Brook, Alabama, everyone goes to college, especially to the University of Alabama or Auburn. But I was pleasantly surprised to learn that everyone "got it."

I asked him to come out on the road and play guitar for me for a while, and it's been awesome. It's surreal to look back and see my son standing on stage playing the songs that he's grown up with his whole life. Some of my band members, like my drummer, Jim Bloodgood, have been with me since Avery was a baby! It won't be for much longer, though, because he has his own band and is pursuing his own career in the music industry.

I'll never forget when Avery was around thirteen years old and we were at the beach on vacation. He and I went out to the water and started talking about his future. I said, "If you decide to pursue music for your life, and you ever date a girl that says, 'It's me or music,' RUN!!!!! Don't ever be with someone who doesn't support your dreams one hundred percent." I also told him that he should spend his twenties building his career, devoting himself to becoming the best musician he can be and making a name for himself, and then, in his thirties, marriage and kids. And then when you're in your forties, I said, take your kids to the beach on vacation. I think that's something that really stuck with him. I tell my girls the same thing.

Avery has been playing guitar since he was about fourteen and has practiced nonstop since then. He is gifted. Truly, truly gifted. Every musical gene that came from my side of the family and from his biological father's side went to Avery. I have never seen anyone learn as fast as he does—and not just learn but master. I knew right when he started that he was going to get it fast, and he has exceeded all my expectations. I think years from now, when we reminisce, we will always talk about how the sound of a very loud electric guitar was the dominating sound pretty much 24/7 in our home. The girls would come downstairs and say, "Mama, tell Avery to turn it down, PLEASE!!!!!!!!!!!!!" But looking back, I miss that sound so much. We still have music at home, though. Livy plays the piano and sings and writes songs in her room. She's just not quite as loud as a guitar amp.

Olivia has inherited the singing gene, and she's amazing. I'm so excited to see what the future holds for her. She is exotically beautiful and just brings people to tears with her voice. She's a better singer than I am.

Audrey is a dancer. She has a great voice, too, and has all the musical abilities that the rest of us do, but she can DANCE, and we can't! At least not like she can. She can pretty much do anything. She's gorgeous and funny and 100 percent an extrovert. I can't even imagine all that she will accomplish. I'm so in love with my girls, and we have such a great bond.

People always ask me if I worry about my kids going into the same career and industry that I am in, and I always say, "No, I would worry more if they didn't." I think it would be awful if none of my kids were interested in music. We relate so much on the subject, and we have deep talks about songs and bands and artists and poetry.

It's the same for Jay and his kids. Three out of his four are extremely talented in sports, just like their daddy. His son Braxton is a quarterback at Alabama; his daughter Sarah Ashlee is a phenomenal basketball player and is committed to the University of Georgia. She has a twin brother named Harrison, and he, too, is a great athlete, the quarterback at his high school. I think it's just natural that kids follow in their parents' footsteps, because they've grown up watching their success and are usually gifted in the same areas.

∞

In 2011, Luke Bryan came out with a song called "Country Girl (Shake It for Me)." That was the beginning of bro-country.

Bro-country has been a time of male country singers dominating the scene and being what country radio wants to play. Most of the songs are about beautiful girls in tight jeans, drinking, partying, down by the river, on a dirt road, under the moonlight, and pickup trucks. For the last eight years, country radio and the music charts have been dominated by male artists who, in my opinion, all sound the same. And every song is manufactured. True substance, great lyrics, and original and beautiful musical sounds are mostly gone from the airwaves. Most important, what is missing from country radio is women.

When I was growing up singing in bars, I would cover all the great female artists: Dolly Parton, Patsy Cline, Loretta Lynn, Tammy Wynette, Reba McEntire, Anne Murray, Patty Loveless, the Judds, and so many more. When I got my record deal, country radio was full of great female artists—like Lee Ann Womack, Trisha Yearwood, Faith Hill, Martina McBride, the Dixie Chicks, LeAnn Rimes, and Wynonna Judd, just to name a few. The music was real and diverse and cool. Now it's just sad to me what has happened to the genre that I once called my home.

Because country radio stopped playing women, it was becoming harder and harder to keep my career going. This was a really tough time for me professionally. I was having to travel a ton to visit radio stations all over the country and perform free shows in hopes that they would play my music. The last song that I released to country radio was "Slow Me Down." That was in 2014. I did something like forty-four free shows that year, on top of my regular touring dates.

No matter what I did, bro-country was all country radio wanted to play. No one seemed to respect all of my previous success that I'd worked years to achieve, and now my hard work and time away from my family were for nothing.

The straw that broke the camel's back was when my manager told me that a radio station wanted me to come and do a free show. Without going into detail, I can say that this would have been extremely difficult and humiliating for me. Finally, I just said, "This is bullshit. I'm not doing this anymore. I can't do this anymore."

I was done.

I had to try something new.

I decided to start my own record label, called Born To Fly Records, and put out music that I think is great and authentic to who I am. This has been so freeing. Now I'm in the driver's seat, and every decision is made between my managers and me. We decide what songs I'm going to record, what photos I'm going to use, what shows I'm going to do, and literally every aspect of my career. I'm so fortunate to have an amazing fan base that enable me to still have a thriving and successful career despite the fact that country radio won't play my new music.

I haven't found the perfect balance in life yet, and that's okay with me. I'm never satisfied, and I'm never done growing and learning and trying new things. Life is always changing, and I love that. I love adventure, and I love knowing that God is in control of my life and that therefore I don't need to worry about a thing. Not worrying is easier said than done, but I really do try, because I know I have control over almost nothing. So why worry? I am so grateful to God for giving me the wiring of an optimist. I really don't like to dwell on the negative, and I don't stay down for very long. I always try to tell myself that everything is fine, and anytime I start feeling anxious, I do two things: pray for others, and count my blessings. It really does work.

I have had a ton of drama in my life, and I have no doubt that there will be more. But it's taught me to fight for the good life, the best life I can have. My goal is to bring joy to people. To make people happy through my music. And to make the people in my sphere happy by loving and serving them well.

Thanks

Cindy Coloma
Craig Dunn
Margaret Riley King
Becky Gardenhire
Trish Townsend
Katherine Cobbs

Index

About the Author

Sara Evans has sold more than seven million albums and has garnered five number one hits on country radio including "A Little Bit Stronger," the title track of her chart-topping 2011 album *Stronger*. The single was number one for two weeks and was certified platinum by the Recording Industry Association of America. Other number one hits include "Born to Fly," "Suds in the Bucket," "A Real Fine Place to Start," and "No Place That Far." Evans continues to bring her music to the fans by touring nationwide, typically performing more than one hundred shows each year. In addition to her music, Evans is an accomplished author of three novels, her memoir *Born to Fly*, and lends her resources and time to many charitable causes, including the CMA Foundation, St. Jude Children's Research Hospital, the American Red Cross, and many more.